'An easy-to-read, practical book, presenting everything needed to facilitate a valuable, therapeutic resource for vulnerable children. A great guide to use for interventions in the primary school.'

– Dawn James, inclusion lead and SENCo

'This is a refreshing book for this moment in education. Through the medium of bricks, Alyson Thomsen explores the developmental and emotional realities of the child with compassion and sensitivity. The structure of the book brings theory and practical ideas together seamlessly. A must-read for reflective and playful educators and parents who want to understand the motivations behind great learning. A gem!'

– Sue Egersdorff, founder and director of International Early Years

'Thera-Build is a truly wonderful therapeutic approach in supporting children's needs. This book is an easy-to-read guide to help practitioners facilitate activities using the medium of LEGO®, specifically targeting areas of need and providing an overall understanding to enable professionals to help stimulate children's imaginations in a playful way in order to reach their true potential.'

– Adriana Sklenar, pastoral support team, Hester's Way Primary School

'This book will definitely have a central place on my bookshelf. As an avid LEGO® builder and child therapist, I am forever seeking ways to combine one of my favourite activities with my vocation. Thera-Build successfully supplied me with a primer full of new ideas and techniques. The book is easy to read and clearly set out. The author assists novice and experienced clinicians, teachers and others working with children to understand the challenges children face. It demonstrates how to build a child's resilience, provide them with a safe and respectful environment and support them.'

– Elsa Struwig, social worker

T0299697

Thera-Build® with LEGO®

of related interest

LEGO®-Based Therapy
How to Build Social Competence through LEGO®-Based Clubs
for Children with Autism and Related Conditions
Daniel B. LeGoff, Gina Gómez de la Cuesta, G.W. Krauss and Simon Baron-Cohen
ISBN 978 1 84905 537 6
eISBN 978 0 85700 960 9

How LEGO®-Based Therapy for Autism Works
Landing on My Planet
Daniel B. LeGoff
ISBN 978 1 78592 710 2
eISBN 978 1 78450 290 4

Building Language Using LEGO® Bricks
A Practical Guide
Dawn Ralph and Jacqui Rochester
Foreword by Gina Gómez de la Cuesta
ISBN 978 1 78592 061 5
eISBN 978 1 78450 317 8

Fun Games and Physical Activities to Help Heal Children Who Hurt
Get On Your Feet!
Beth Powell
ISBN 978 1 78592 773 7
eISBN 978 1 78450 678 0

Parenting with Theraplay®
Understanding Attachment and How to Nurture
a Closer Relationship with Your Child
Vivien Norris and Helen Rodwell
Forewords by Phyllis Booth and Dafna Lender
ISBN 978 1 78592 209 1
eISBN 978 1 78450 489 2

Thera-Build® with LEGO®

A Playful Therapeutic Approach for Promoting Emotional Well-Being in Children

Alyson Thomsen

Jessica Kingsley *Publishers*
London and Philadelphia

First published in 2018
by Jessica Kingsley Publishers
73 Collier Street
London N1 9BE, UK
and
400 Market Street, Suite 400
Philadelphia, PA 19106, USA

www.jkp.com

Library of Congress Cataloging in Publication Data
A CIP catalog record for this book is available from the Library of Congress

British Library Cataloguing in Publication Data
A CIP catalogue record for this book is available from the British Library

ISBN 978 1 78592 492 7
eISBN 978 1 78450 881 4

Printed and bound in Great Britain

Dedication

I dedicate this book to my three boys: Lasse, James and Oliver,
without whom, none of this would have been possible.
I love you all unconditionally, and am thankful to be part of your team.

Acknowledgements

I would like to thank Hannah Clarke for her influence on my professional development, and for recognising the value of 'Thera-Build' as an effective intervention.

My warmest thanks to Alex and Rachel Henderson, who insisted that this book be written, and supportively read each chapter with such interest and enthusiasm.

Finally, my thanks and very best wishes to all the children who have travelled along with me on the 'Thera-Build' journey. You are all unique, special and amazing young people, and I feel privileged to have been able to play, talk and build with you.

Disclaimer

LEGO®, the LEGO® logo, the Brick and Knob configurations and the Minifigure are trademarks of the LEGO® Group, which does not sponsor, authorise or endorse this book.

Contents

Preface

Thera-Build is my brainchild, Alyson Thomsen, a former senior teacher and LEGO® Education Certified Trainer in the UK. I hope that you find it useful.

Our family was relocated to Denmark in 2008, then on to Colorado, USA in 2010, following my husband's employment with LEGO® Systems, which is when my relationship with bricks began.

Upon our return to the UK in 2012, I was keen to head back to the classroom part-time, using LEGO® to boost academic performance. Whole-class literacy and science, technology, engineering and mathematics (STEM) activities were particularly popular; however, as the months went by, I increasingly spent time working with small groups of targeted children, for whom academic challenges were just one area of concern.

I realised that in order for the children in my focus groups to reach their academic potential, they needed more social and emotional support; so, I set about reading, researching and training in this area. Bringing a more therapeutic approach into the classroom and combining it with LEGO® building activities seemed to be delivering positive outcomes, in terms of well-being, behaviour and greater academic success.

In 2015 the concept of 'Thera-Build' was conceived, and I set about trialling and developing my ideas. By 2016 it was established as a successful intervention, based on empirical evidence from the schools, charities and trusts that had commissioned projects, and Thera-Build became the main focus of my work.

I continue to work as a Thera-Build practitioner, offering one-to-one and group sessions with children and young people. I also provide training courses for parents, carers and professionals. This book seemed to be the next logical step. For more information on Thera-Build training, please visit www.bricks2learn.com/thera-build/training.

Chapter 1

Thera-Build

INTRODUCTION AND FUNDAMENTALS

Introduction

Thera-Build is a therapeutic programme for building confidence and self-esteem using LEGO®. It is based on playful, active interaction with children and young people, to improve social skills, build resilience and promote good mental health.

If a child does not enjoy using LEGO® as a medium, it should not be forced upon them. LEGO® is first and foremost a toy, and must be preserved as such.

A playful facilitator who finds joy in building with LEGO® is best placed for implementing Thera-Build.

What should I expect from this book?

This practical resource offers a complete insight into the Thera-Build programme. It contains:

- the theory behind the methodology
- helpful strategies for developing sessions
- effective ways of organising, monitoring and assessing sessions
- tried and tested LEGO® activities
- LEGO® building tips and ideas
- real-life case stories
- practical advice on resourcing, storage and cleaning.

What sort of difficulties can be addressed through a Thera-Build approach?

Referrals to the Thera-Build programme fall into two main, interconnected categories:

1. A child is displaying behaviours that are causing concern:
   i. angry and aggressive outbursts
   ii. bullying or being bullied
   iii. quiet and withdrawn
   iv. raised anxiety levels
   v. signs of self-harm.

2. A specific incident has occurred in a child's life that may require a therapeutic response:
   i. domestic violence
   ii. separation/divorce/imprisonment/abandonment
   iii. long-term/terminal illness

iv. substance abuse

v. death of a family member/grief.

If a child's needs are too complex for a Thera-Build intervention, they should be referred on to a clinical consultant for expert advice, assessment and therapy.

Is Thera-Build realistic in an educational setting?

I am often asked whether a therapeutic approach is appropriate in a school environment. More specifically about how issues of discipline, boundaries and control will be addressed, when the children are clearly having a lovely time playing with LEGO®, and not apparently learning anything of any educational value.

As a former senior teacher, I do understand the pressures schools face in terms of inspections, exam results, league tables and dwindling budgets; demands that make it difficult to justify a playful intervention in which children are not directly involved in academic activity. I also accept the argument that teachers are not social workers or therapists. However, many teachers and support workers are already dealing daily with children whose knee-jerk response to new challenges is to lash out verbally or physically, or to go into defiant withdrawal.

Children who have experienced early childhood trauma are highly unlikely to be brought to reason by a verbal reprimand, the threat of a more senior staff member being sent for, a call home to a parent, or even exclusion when in a mental state of hyper or hypo arousal. Aggressive outbursts or refusal to comply usually result in punishment of one kind or another, which may temporarily put a stop to the behaviours. However, they are certain to be repeated when a child is triggered, because the underlying alarm system is still on, scanning for danger, and prepared to re-activate at the slightest provocation. We need to work with children to get this internal system under control, so that a child is able to access the curriculum, engage with the teaching staff and reach their full potential.

I am frequently told that a child 'can behave when they want to' and therefore if they do not respond at a particular moment in time to what is expected of them, or adhere to what is considered appropriate or acceptable right there and then, they are 'just being naughty'. This is a challenge, but it is part and parcel of the fallout of childhood trauma, and labelling the child as a problem will in all probability exacerbate the behaviour, as the child assumes the role that they have been allocated.

With disapproving judgements, low expectations and a sense of not belonging, there is absolutely no incentive, indeed little point, in trying to change the tide of public opinion against them. Children in this situation may well give up trying, withdraw and refuse to engage, or become more defiant and aggressive in line with expectations. For children who have been the victims of complex trauma, this creates yet another level of complication.

It is well understood that pupils cannot learn effectively without good mental health. Maybe, just maybe, there is an alternative approach which recognises that school can offer a place of safety for children who have experienced, or are still living with, traumatic stress. A space in which they can make sense of what has happened/ is happening in their chaotic lives, and that offers them a lifeline, a way of being meaningfully connected, so that they can begin to build healthy relationships where they are supported to access the education that is being offered to them.

Thera-Build fundamentals

Thera-Build is an adult-led but child-centred programme that is completely responsive to the individual needs of each child.

Practitioners facilitate the building process by giving the child the tools for successful construction, for example how to follow a build-guide, use a brick separator, understand LEGO® measurements and technical vocabulary. They also guide children through the building process, offering help and support where appropriate, but not controlling the finished outcome.

The main emphasis, however, is on the process rather than the product. The practitioner should ensure that children feel safe and secure in a session, that they are seen and listened to, and given opportunities for meaningful conversation(s) in order to build positive relationships.

Practitioners must:

- ensure that every child feels safe, valued and accepted for who they are

- be responsive to individual needs and recognise every child's potential

- create LEGO® building experiences that help children thrive

- provide high-quality relational experiences to help children connect, to feel that they belong

- structure sessions to provide safety and regulation

- inspire, motivate, be flexible in plans and responses, so that spontaneous play can flourish

- support and extend children's building skills and imaginative processes

- be fully present on a building project, to help children to become better integrated

- attune to the rhythm, energy and pace of each child

- be playful, explore, create, imagine, relax and laugh together through co-construction

- interact with sensitivity, valuing children's ideas and contributions

- build confidence by doing, and let the feelings follow on

- not judge: 'I don't like what you did, but I do like you'

- give children 'permission' to get it wrong – if they don't like a model, they can change it!

- encourage a higher level of understanding through discussion, negotiation and compromise.

Thera-Build process

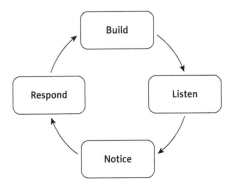

Build

- Thera-Build relies on the physical connection with LEGO® bricks to support self-regulation.

- Engage in the construction process together, to create and model a healthy, positive, caring relationship.

- Select appropriately sized and themed bricks, to generate a successful, enjoyable building experience.

- Build safety and trust to help a child relax. They are then more likely to talk about any underlying anxieties.

- The action of playful building can take the pressure off talking face to face.

- When building, 'wondering aloud' can be a helpful technique in floating thoughts and encouraging conversation: 'I wonder what you are thinking…', 'I wonder how that felt for you…', 'I wonder if things changed…', 'I wonder what you might say to another child if…'

Listen

- I am here with you, and I hear you!

- Concentrate on listening, rather than sharing experiences, or offering advice.

- Use 'active listening' to try to understand what the behaviour is communicating; listening both to what is actually said and what is not being said.

- It may help to summarise what you think you have understood as a conversation continues.

- Ask 'open' questions that require more than a monosyllabic response.

- Mirror empathy: 'I can see/hear how hurt you are. Tell me more about…'

Notice

- Be curious and pay attention to the child.

- Be aware of their base-line level of arousal, potential triggers and their window of tolerance.

- Notice any changes in facial expression or voice modulation, sudden body movements or repetitive actions.

- Children will use a variety of behaviours to communicate their needs, for example, shouting, kicking, withdrawing. What is the message they are trying to communicate? Notice me, hear me, understand me, help me?

- Look out for defensive behaviours. They are generally used for self-protection and might have helped to keep a child safe in the past.

- Use 'check-in' activities to encourage a child to communicate their feelings. When a child does not know how or what they feel, it's usually a conflict of emotions. Bear in mind that it is the darkest feelings which no one else wants to hear that most need our understanding, for example, grief, futility, rage, and shame.

Respond

- Having your attention, and feeling liked by you, is hugely important for a child's mental health.

- Feeling understood can make a situation feel more bearable, even without a solution. It is also more likely to precipitate a positive change in behaviour.

- Say less rather than more and avoid platitudes – they are not very consoling for anyone going through a tough time.

- Encourage the narrative, for example, what happened next? Use conjunctions, for example, because? Then…

- Try not to panic or appear shocked, when something is disclosed.

- Practitioners must not promise complete confidentiality.

Thera-Build mantra (the four Ss)

The children and young people in our care need to be:

Seen: This means perceiving them deeply and empathically.

Safe: Specifically avoiding actions and responses that might frighten or hurt them.

Secure: Supporting, developing, nurturing an internalised sense of well-being and self-worth.

Soothed: Helping them to deal with difficult emotions or challenging situations, so that they can learn resilience and the ability to self-soothe.

Therapeutic aims

- Create a sense of belonging and connection.
- Reduce stress and generate greater calm and relaxation.
- Improve ability to self-regulate and self-soothe.
- Encourage empathy.
- Strengthen trust in others.
- Increase resilience and enhance self-esteem.
- Support a more confident and optimistic outlook on life.
- Bring about greater self-awareness.
- Promote expression and improve social skills.
- Develop self-reliance and personal responsibility.

Thera-Build essentials

There are four important factors to remember when implementing a Thera-Build intervention:

Building relationships

Thera-Build aims to develop a nurturing bond between the child and practitioner. It also provides opportunities for collaboration, teamwork and conflict resolution with other children. In order to help the children in our care to build positive social connections and healthy relationships, we must convey the message that 'You are worth my time. You are a valuable person.'

It is our responses to children, as well as the encounters and inevitable difficulties they face, that help them to make sense of the world and learn from these experiences; so, create building opportunities that help children thrive, be patient and encouraging, praise their achievements and be excited about their discoveries!

Movement

Where practical, the Thera-Build programme favours movement. A small amount of physical activity is undertaken when sorting through boxes to find the correct elements and when actually building. It is important, however, to allow children to change position and to be comfortable. You don't have to build sitting on a chair with the LEGO® on a table. Move it onto the floor and let the child lay on their side, stretch out on their tummy, or assume a genie position.

When planning a session, consider how a child might need and want to move about quite naturally. For example, racing cars down a ramp involves the child launching their vehicle from the top and moving the length of the ramp to retrieve it.

Splitting a session into parts is a helpful way of bringing about purposeful movement. By starting with a game and then moving to a free-build for instance, a different part of the room could be utilised, and different furniture.

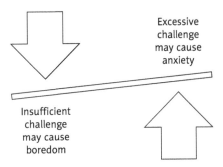

Excessive challenge may cause anxiety

Insufficient challenge may cause boredom

Flow

Thera-Build practitioners should aim for good 'flow' when interacting with children. This is a wonderfully mindful and powerful building state where a child is relaxed, connected to the process and most likely to talk openly.

Dialogue should be natural and a child should never be forced into a discussion. Silence is often necessary for concentration and creativity.

Confidentiality

As a rapport is built through the Thera-Build programme and children feel safe enough to begin to share their thoughts and experiences, issues of trust and confidentiality may arise. Whilst I would never want to break a child's confidence, responsibility for their overall care and protection must take precedence.

Treat all conversations as confidential, unless a disclosure leads to the belief that a child might not be safe; in which case, sharing that information with the appropriate agencies is mandatory. Keep records of all meetings.

Always be familiar with and adhere to the child protection and safeguarding policies in each individual setting.

Chapter 2

Why LEGO®? And the Importance of Play

The power of play

At its core, the Thera-Build programme is based around the power of playing with LEGO®. Play is absolutely essential for the healthy development and well-being of all of our children. Through play children learn about themselves, others and the world around them.

Play allows young people to learn through trial and error, in a safe and relaxed manner, making connections with past learning, and transferring knowledge and understanding to new areas of exploration. It is important to remember that play, a psychological, biological and social necessity, is an investment in a child, and is as important for the developmental needs of all children as warmth, protection and nutrition.

The play deficit

There does seem to be significant concern that children 'don't play like they used to', that play no longer seems to come naturally or spontaneously, and that children don't regularly amuse themselves outside with friends, preferring instead to spend their time inside, gaming alone, on tablets, consoles or computers.

Many adults are concerned that they do not know how to play with their children, that they have grown up and left their playful selves behind, forgetting how to connect with that part of themselves, and somehow having lost the 'art' of play. Work commitments, household responsibilities and homework demands put an increasing strain on families, resulting in less time and energy for play, which becomes downgraded to a low priority, something to do when everything else has been done!

Widespread materialism seems at odds with creating the right conditions for children's emotional needs to be met. As child psychologist David Elkind (2007, p.27) points out, 'Children in the twenty-first [century] have been transformed from net producers of their own toy and play culture to net consumers of a play culture imposed by adults.'

Fear for children's safety and welfare means that adults are increasingly wanting to manage their child's movements and control their playground and after-school activities. The ever-increasing demands from school, coupled with test preparation or extra tuition, encroach upon children's free time. Often, sadly, break times and lunch times are crammed with catch-up classes, meetings or detentions, which detract from the time that children should be spending playing outside, engaging in naturally self-generated social play.

The innate need for children to learn, be curious, imagine and take risks is becoming eroded by an over-scheduling, commercialised and increasingly technological culture which lacks the creative play experiences that our youngsters so desperately need.

Children's learning should be stimulated and enriched by playful encounters that are relevant, inventive and resourceful, providing them with rich, fertile opportunities to explore, imagine and experiment, and opening young minds to new possibilities and discoveries.

What is play?

Play is supposed to be a pleasure-filled activity and doesn't have to cost anything monetarily. Play can be found in a woodland walk, in the making of homemade gloop, or inside an empty cardboard box!

Children love to have the undivided attention of a playful, attentive adult for a period of time, allowing them to receive the message that they are precious, liked and valued. Play:

- allows children to explore and express ideas, emotions and feelings

- provides opportunities for social contact with others

- enables children to relax

- contributes to their all-round intellectual growth

- develops resilience and perseverance

- bolsters self-esteem and self-confidence

- may be creative, constructive, imaginative and physical.

Play progression

The Thera-Build methodology relies on practitioners operating as facilitators; interacting socially and playing side-by-side with children. Enough support, stimulation and challenge should be offered to help a child to improve their own skill level as independently as possible, to ignite their imagination and to increase their self-esteem and levels of confidence.

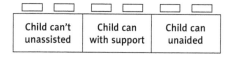

Child can't unassisted	Child can with support	Child can unaided

Emotional and cognitive development through play

The research evidence is overwhelming in documenting the power of play for children's emotional well-being, social development and academic achievement.

With increasing emphasis on the mental health and well-being of our children, Thera-Build offers plenty of creative, self-directed play opportunities for children to initiate their own building experiences and invent their own worlds.

Studies have shown that children who are involved with plenty of creative, self-directed, exploratory play experiences develop much more resilience and are better able to regulate their own emotions and behaviour, when compared to other children. Thus, play is not time wasted that could be better spent on other pursuits; play has tremendous value.

Play development

The classic study of how play develops in children was carried out by Mildred Parten in the late 1920s, at the Institute of Child Development in Minnesota. Whilst more contemporary variations have been established, Parten's Stages of Play are still extensively used today. They detail how children are more likely to move away from more solitary play into social play, as they mature, interact with their peers and improve their communication skills.

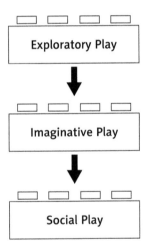

Structured free-play

Structured free-play is the Thera-Build way to play.

Children are given clean, safe and age-appropriate bricks that they can hold and manipulate successfully and that really appeal to them. There is a loose thematic structure to the building process, but the emphasis is to put minimal restrictions on their creativity, and to give the children as much freedom as possible during the session. Playing is an end in itself, with no obvious goal or conclusion.

Each model should be celebrated on its own merits and the emphasis is on originality and individuality, not on building the perfect model or using an element in the conventional way. On the contrary, I absolutely love it when a child uses a brick in a way I have never thought of!

Give them opportunities to think for themselves and to make choices. Who minds if a tree is orange? If a child tells me it's a tree, then it is! I might take the opportunity to ask why it is orange, to tap into a child's thought processes and creativity. After all, it could be a lava, goldfish or orange juice tree, which could take the narrative along on a wonderful new tangent.

Thera-Build provides play in a safe environment in which children can experiment and build. One of the particular benefits of LEGO® is that if you want to make a change, you can, relatively easily, without ruining the whole model. Children are free to build as they choose, to express themselves with the bricks and to derive happiness or pride from their creations, which they are then free to play with.

Thera-Build is playful

I value play highly. It can be infectious, inspiring, entertaining and liberating. Playful connections bring such joy to child and practitioner alike, and really generate positive connections and successful relationships. Play becomes a vehicle for learning in its own right.

At times, it may not be appropriate to overtly laugh and joke with a child, but purposeful play is always on the Thera-Build menu. After all, creativity and imagination are like muscles: if you don't use them, you lose them.

The developmental stages of brick play

When playing with bricks, children are free to reconstruct their own experiences and to engage in activities that they are excluded from in reality, such as driving a tractor, flying a plane or escaping a zombie apocalypse.

Building with bricks is a really valuable learning experience for children to stimulate their creativity and imagination, to help them to develop their fine and gross motor skills, and to improve spatial awareness.

Although no single progression would be accepted as definitive, young children typically go through these stages when playing with bricks:

Brick play progression

Approximate age	Expected brick play progression
1–2 years	• Touch, hold, feel, lick and chew on bricks • Bang bricks together, making a noise • Drop or throw bricks • Carry bricks around, pile them into collections • Begin to click two or three bricks together
2–3 years	• Stack bricks vertically or horizontally, using both hands to build • Search for hidden bricks • Create and purposefully demolish structures • Show interest in brick features, for example, a hinged door or window

3–4 years	• Combine building plates to make roads
	• Build simple vehicles and include Minifigures in play
	• Join bricks together to make a recognisable structure, for example, a bridge
	• Group bricks by colour, size or shape and count them
4–5 years	• Build simple houses
	• Engage in more open-ended, exploratory building
	• Use bricks to build an enclosed space such as a farm or park
	• Create symmetrical structures and patterns
	• Name their models during or after construction
	• Build co-operatively with peers, towards a common goal
5+ years	• Plan what they intend to build before starting a model
	• Use bricks to represent real scenarios, places or things
	• Build elaborate structures, adding detailed elements to the build
	• Include others in the construction process, with assigned roles
	• Play imaginatively with the structure, creating stories with the bricks

Why LEGO®?

At the core of the Thera-Build methodology is the use of LEGO® as a therapeutic tool. LEGO® itself has no particular magical qualities or special powers, but it is a wonderfully creative building system that has significant therapeutic value, when used correctly. Whilst Thera-Build can be adapted to be used with other toys – the programme, after all, is designed to help build relationships and understanding – it is based on the LEGO® system because of the exceptional quality, durability and adaptability of the LEGO® product range.

- It is an excellent tool for providing sensory stimulation over which a child can have control.

- It is high quality, predictable and versatile.

- LEGO® is compatible with DUPLO® and still works together with bricks going back generations.

- It is recognised worldwide by its playful attributes as a toy. Let's keep it that way!

LEGO® is a brand name and not a collective noun for all plastic bricks

Thera-Build is not sponsored or authorised by the LEGO® Group, but it is important to point out that not all plastic bricks are made equally!

A collection of toy bricks will often be referred to as 'LEGOs', which is incorrect. The word LEGO® is a brand name, and therefore should be referred to as an adjective, and not a noun, for example, 'LEGO® bricks'.

Consumers need to make buying decisions on an informed basis and, whilst there are many cheaper replicas on the market, offering 'more bricks for your buck', they are not of the same high quality or durability as genuine LEGO® elements, and this could make for a disappointing or frustrating build.

As the Thera-Build programme aims to create building experiences that help children thrive, we must provide a quality tool to support this process. Unfortunately, there is a cost to buying the best, but remember that whilst LEGO® is expensive, it is long-lasting and generations of children may benefit from the initial investment.

How do I select a LEGO® set?

LEGO® is so well designed and thoroughly tested on children that it makes sense to follow the official age rating provided on the box. In order to keep in flow, it is important that a challenge does not become too great for a child. It is very unlikely that the dexterity required for a 12+ LEGO® Architecture model, for instance, would be appropriate for a 6-year-old child, as the elements in the build are very small and difficult to manoeuvre without the acquired fine motor skills.

Thera-Build responds to the needs and building ability of individual children; however, it is important not to impose limits on a child who has the skill and the eagerness to construct more complex models.

It can also be tremendous fun to provide older age groups with bricks designed for pre-schoolers.

The activity should determine the best bricks to use.

LEGO® product progression

0–3 years	LEGO® DUPLO®	Bricks are twice the size of classic LEGO® bricks, making them perfect for small hands
2+ years	LEGO® Soft Brick Set	Large, flexible and spongy bricks in four basic colours
3–5 years	LEGO® Juniors	Regular-sized bricks, but containing pre-made elements, making models easier to construct. A great introduction to building with classic bricks
5–12 years	LEGO® City LEGO® Classic LEGO® Creator	All regular-sized bricks. Mixed boxes or specific sets, providing realistic LEGO® World models
7–12 years	LEGO® Boost	Combines standard building bricks with coding, using a free downloadable app. A tablet is required to control and program this product
7–14 years	LEGO® Technic	Provides a challenge for experienced LEGO® builders, using pegs and beams to build real-life functions, such as gearboxes, steering systems and suspension

cont.

10+ years	LEGO® MINDSTORMS®	A mix of Classic bricks and Technic elements combined to build and program walking, talking and thinking robots!
12+ years	LEGO® Architecture	Iconic buildings from around the world, built in smaller elements from the classic brick range

Other LEGO® themes

It is of absolute importance that building activities are based around a child's individual interests. An initial Thera-Build session involves a variety of different elements, in order to observe and talk with the child at play, and thereby gain a clearer picture of the child's interests and building ability.

From this session, both child and practitioner can discuss future activities together, and the adult can prepare and excite the child about subsequent sessions.

There are many 'evergreen' themes such as space, castles and dinosaurs that are continuously popular. Other themes that have experienced longevity in the product range are LEGO® STAR WARS™ and LEGO® Friends. Thera-Build also taps into popular culture with themes such as Minecraft™ and Disney's Frozen™, or takes a particular character or building to develop, for example, Rapunzel's Tower or Batman's Cave.

It is vitally important that the LEGO® project is set at an appropriate level for the child's building ability. The age guide on the box is useful intel, but a practitioner must know the individual they are working with, and ensure that the build experience is manageable.

Prepare to join in and interact in a meaningful and sensitive way; but do not dominate the build, as adult-initiated play can often have precise aims and objectives that are at odds with a child's creative processes. By all means establish an exciting environment, listen to the ideas of the child and suggest challenges, different brick choices or building suggestions to enhance their play experience; but a practitioner should not impose their recommendations and, when the child is in flow, should know when to leave a child be, to develop their own play experience.

The benefits of brick play

COGNITIVE	PHYSICAL
Language + literacy skills Mathematical + scientific reasoning Problem-solving Decision-making Thoughts and memory	Fine and gross motor skills Hand-eye coordination Spatial awareness Sensory concepts Managing stress
EMOTIONAL	SOCIAL
Self-confidence and self-reliance Self-regulation/impulse control Persistence and resilience Self-awareness Empathy	Positive communication Co-operation and collaboration Self-expression Negotiation and compromise Rule formation and leadership

Chapter 3

The Brain Science Behind Thera-Build

Brain plasticity

Brain plasticity is a term used by neuroscientists that refers to the brain's ability to change throughout life, for both better and worse. Biology, environment and experience all play a significant role in human brain plasticity.

Neuroscientists had previously believed that the brain developed all its major functionality in early infancy and that, as we aged, the connections in the brain became fixed. However, recent pioneering experiments have shown that the human brain is in fact capable of incredible change, and that it has the ability to reorganise itself by forming new connections. It can adapt, compensate for damage, renew itself and heal, by generating new neurons and creating neural pathways, even into old age. This 'plasticity' plays an incredibly important role in brain development, and in shaping distinct personalities.

Left hemisphere	The corpus callosum	Right hemisphere
Logical		Creative
Analytical		Imaginative
Rational		Intuitive
Sequential		Perceptive
Objective		Subjective
Science		Art
Maths		Music
Language		Fantasy
Factual		Abstract
Reasoning		Emotions

Brain integration

The brain is divided into two hemispheres, with each half performing a fairly distinct set of operations. Generally speaking, left-brain thinking is verbal and analytical, controlling many aspects of language and logic, whereas the right brain is non-verbal and holistic, more intuitive and able to facilitate emotions.

The corpus callosum is the part of the mind that allows communication between the two hemispheres of the brain. It is responsible for transmitting neural messages between both the right-brain emotions and the left-brain logic, to bring about a well-functioning whole.

We need both sides of the brain to connect to each other, linking the separate specialist parts and integrating the whole brain system in order to thrive. Integration coordinates the two hemispheres, allowing access to our emotions and creativity in a healthy, balanced and considered way.

Whilst we may have a natural tendency towards one way of thinking, the two sides of our brain work together in our everyday lives, and children can only fully realise their potential by activating both sides of their brain. By consciously activating the power of each hemisphere on a regular basis, and using both parts of the brain together, a child will become more integrated, which should improve their mental health and increase their academic potential.

How does LEGO® support brain integration?

Basic brain architecture and innate temperament have a significant effect on the way that a brain develops; but everything that happens to us changes the physical structure of the brain, so the good news is that it is possible to positively rewire it.

Play, for instance, has a profound effect in creating new neural connections in the brain. The combination of physical construction activities and imaginative, creative play mirrors the integration of left- and right-brain hemispheres, resulting in greater balance and healthy well-being.

By providing building experiences that consciously activate the power of each hemisphere, then combining these skills in a playful style, children are able to make stronger brain connections and move towards greater self-control and resilience.

Integrating the brain should help to support a securer attachment style, which in turn should increase confidence, improve socialisation skills and help develop a resilient child who can thrive socially, emotionally and intellectually.

When free-building with LEGO®, we of course, tap into our imagination and creativity and connect with the abstract, which exercises the right-brain hemisphere.

The left-brain hemisphere is given a good work out when we follow the sequential process of adhering to a build guide, or working on a problem-solving activity.

Mental health for all

Good mental health begins in infancy, and yet many of our children, for a whole host of reasons, are now living vulnerable lives, which require either direct interventions or care from the state.

It is estimated that one in ten children in the UK have a diagnosable mental health disorder, which equates to approximately three children in every class.

Left undetected or allowed to take root, the impact of mental ill health on a child will undoubtedly go on to have a direct, negative influence on their adult mental state. It therefore makes perfect sense to tackle issues as early and swiftly as possible.

I advocate that mental health education should be a compulsory part of the curriculum in all schools, for all children.

Whilst it is vitally important to provide immediate resources for young people who are already showing signs of mental ill health or are at greater risk, it is imperative that all children are taught about and helped to understand what mental health actually is, and how it can be nurtured and protected. Young people should be equipped with the skills to cultivate their own mental well-being, given the tools with which to best assist themselves and their peers, the information to recognise the warning signs and symptoms of potential problems, and the knowledge of where and how to access help when it is needed, at an age-appropriate level.

Our current infrastructure is creaking under the pressure of the global mental health crisis, and few will escape its effects, even if they are not directly touched by an episode of mental ill health themselves. Many adults with mental health issues can trace their symptoms back to childhood. Thus, it makes sense to aim for prevention, or early intervention, before mental health difficulties really take hold. If they are left untreated, there is a risk that children and young people will fall behind at school, get into trouble with the law, have difficulty getting and holding down a job, face homelessness and their physical health will suffer too, possibly resulting in substance abuse and early death.

Unresolved mental health problems lie at the heart of some of our greatest social challenges, so we must begin to break the cycle, end the stigma and educate society about mental health.

What is stress?

Stress is primarily a physical response brought about by a state of mental/emotional strain or tension. Stress can be a really positive thing: it can be motivating, challenging, exciting and extremely helpful for survival when faced with a dangerous situation.

However, when overstressed and the body thinks it is under permanent attack, stress has a very negative impact on the body, which can be extremely detrimental to both mental and physical health. Many of our young people are entering school already suffering with stress-related conditions, making it difficult for them to learn. An education system that is following an increasingly narrow, academic curriculum, which is target-driven, relying on endless testing and assessment, and failing to instil emotional intelligence, is not conducive to good mental health.

How stress affects the brain

Stress over a period of time can lead to changes in the parts of the brain that control and manage feelings. This can have long-term effects on physical, mental and emotional growth. Early trauma may affect a child's nervous system, which is largely shaped by the child's experiences and the responses received from those around them, as the child tries to make sense of the world.

It is truly shocking to hear evidence that stress *in utero* may harmfully impact a foetus, and that the body chemistry of a child growing up in a stressful setting will show significantly higher levels of the hormone cortisol, which is secreted in response to perceived threats, than for a child whose early life was more settled and predictable.

Stress provokes the brain to instruct the adrenal glands to secrete cortisol, which can be a life-saving response in a dangerous or threatening situation in the short term. However, prolonged exposure to high levels of cortisol has physiologically damaging effects. Cortisol hinders the growth of new neurons, and remaining neurons are vulnerable to toxicity as a result of overstimulation. Maintenance of this state therefore actually impairs long-term survival and quality of life, as the brain cannot adapt, modify its response, form new neurons or develop new connections.

The fight/flight/freeze response

The fight, flight, freeze responses are the main human, primitive and powerful survival reactions to imminent threat.

Fight

When the body becomes stressed, resulting in agitation and aggressiveness towards others. This might be a helpful reaction when warding off a predator, but can affect relationships negatively, and damage reputations.

Flight

When the body becomes stressed, resulting in running away from a situation. This might be a helpful reaction when fleeing from a blazing car, but can make an already stressful state much worse, as that stressor will still exist and need to be confronted.

Freeze

When the body becomes stressed, resulting in paralysis. This might be a helpful reaction when 'playing dead' in the hope that a predator will lose interest and wander off; but is frequently a sign of being so overwhelmed, with the energy generated by the perceived threat becoming locked into the nervous system, that the body becomes immobilised.

How does stress affect behaviour?

Ideally when a child's fight/flight/freeze response is triggered, it will return to equilibrium once the threat has been downgraded. In the traumatised child, however, stress hormones continue to be released and don't return to normal levels. They get stuck in fight/flight/freeze mode, which is when we might expect to see behaviours representative of either extreme agitation, or complete collapse. The brain cannot reason when it is overwhelmed by fear, anxiety or anger, so children need to be supported in regulating their moods and emotions.

How does stress affect learning?

When a child is stressed, the cognitive ability to think and make positive choices is physically blocked. No amount of reasoning, shouting or deal-making will work, as the amygdala is in control, responding to the threat and in full survival mode. Children may defensively block out any neglect or abuse, pretending that they don't care, but that imprint remains rather like a permanent tattoo, leaving both the body and brain on high alert, preparing to protect and defend themselves.

When emotions are raging out of control the fight/flight/freeze response will be activated and physical and behavioural changes should be anticipated.

We know that high levels of stress and anxiety can trigger aggressive behaviour, but it is our response to the outbursts that we need to consider also, as this has a dramatic effect on outcomes. It can be challenging, as our own amygdala may well become aroused by a verbal attack, or angry outburst, so we have to cope with our own reaction as practitioners, as well as that of a highly aroused child.

Simple Neuroscience

PREFRONTAL CORTEX
The 'Thinking' Part
Helping us make good,
well-balanced choices

HIPPOCAMPUS
The 'Making Sense'
Part
Storing and recalling
memories

AMYGDALA
The 'Primitive Fear'
Response
Trying to protect us

When the AMYGDALA responds to a real, or perceived threat,
the HIPPOCAMPUS becomes overwhelmed and the
PREFRONTAL CORTEX stops working properly.

In a school setting, there are rules to obey, behaviour policies and plans to follow, other children and members of staff watching on and parents to appease, so it is incredibly difficult, and indeed brave, to take an individual child-centred approach to behaviour, to look for the effects of stress and trauma on a child and to react with sensitivity, empathy and acceptance.

It is not always easy, but I work on the basis that misbehaviour assumes the child made a choice about the way they acted, and could have done it differently. If, at the time of an incident, the child rationally explains the actions taken and the motivation for their response, then this strongly suggests it was an informed reaction.

Stress behaviour, however, is physiologically based, and therefore not a deliberate choice. The child may well not be rationally aware of what they are doing, or have done. They may also be incredibly embarrassed, even shamed by their behaviour, when they have had time to calm down and reflect, because the outburst was so sudden, powerful and perhaps shocking.

How can Thera-Build help?

It stands to reason that a child who is truly loved and well looked after can play, explore, co-operate and problem-solve safely. When this is not the case and a child grows up fearful or neglected, then the brain has to adapt to manage that terror and isolation, and whilst constantly defending itself, does not have the capacity to learn, to play or even to imagine and be creative.

If experience shapes the brain, 'Neurons that fire together wire together' (Siegel and Payne Bryson 2012), then we must provide encounters that can restore feelings of safety, that encourage healthy ways of responding to and with others, and that help bring about emotional self-regulation, because the need for attachment and connection does not diminish.

The whole Thera-Build methodology is based around creating security, and even young children are able to understand some basic principles about the workings of the brain, which in turn helps them to understand their feelings and behaviours. Thera-Build aims to address these both implicitly and explicitly, assisting children by offering repeated experiences that create connections between different parts to develop the whole brain, with the intention of nurturing stronger, more resilient children, and explicitly teaching simple brain functions and physical responses to stimuli.

The ability of a child to regulate their behaviour largely hinges upon their ability to manage stress. Consider the themes of academic pressure, friendship issues, family tensions, social conformity, religious demands, negative behaviour cycles, financial concerns and health worries, as some of the potential sources of stress, making it hard for children and young people to focus on their schoolwork.

It is in everyone's best interests to reduce that tension and allow a child time to recover from their exhaustion when their stress load gets too great. See www.build-happy.co.uk for the '5 Ways to Well-Being' resource and upcoming training dates (Thomsen and Green 2017).

Chapter 4

Thera-Build, Early Childhood Trauma and Attachment

Early childhood trauma

Trauma occurs when a child has an experience or repeated experiences that leave them feeling unsafe and overwhelmingly fearful. Trauma isn't just an event that occurred in the past, it is the child's internal response to the external circumstances, the imprint left by the experience on the brain.

Early childhood trauma usually refers to traumatic experience(s) which occur before the age of six years that significantly impact a child. This includes trauma/abuse that was experienced as a very young infant, before language skills were developed (pre-verbal) and may well have had a detrimental effect on normal brain development.

When children are unable to process the trauma they have experienced, and cope with the difficulties that have arisen, it can stifle their continued development. Children need help to understand and come to terms with their experience, to bring about future positive change.

Common traumas

- accidents
- loss: divorce, death, abandonment
- violence in the home and community
- illness: physical and mental

- separation: imprisonment, military deployment, foster placement
- bullying
- substance misuse
- terrorism
- natural disasters
- abuse: physical, sexual, emotional, psychological, neglect.

The effects of trauma

Children who have grown up in an environment where they have not felt safe, and where care-giving has at best been inadequate, find their own ways of dealing with the anxiety, helplessness and rage that overwhelm them, and the unpleasant physical sensations that they live with as a result. The more frequent and severe the trauma, the more likely that problems will emerge.

Some of the possible symptoms include irritability, sleep difficulties, impulsivity, the inability to be soothed or comforted, unusually high levels of anger, fear of separation, changes in eating patterns, controlling conduct and difficulty making friends. Behaviours such as head-banging, throwing tantrums, kicking doors, bolting and hiding, selective mutism or bedwetting may arise, and as children grow older they may try to numb their feelings still further with drug misuse, violence or sexual contact.

Too traumatised to learn

We know that trauma can affect a child's ability to learn, particularly when they are in a dysregulated state, but trauma may also affect the imagination, without which children cannot envision new possibilities and thus lack hope – a very bleak outlook on life.

Chronic abuse and neglect in childhood interfere with the wiring of sensory integration systems, which can lead on to problems with hand–eye coordination, difficulties following instructions because of faulty connections, delays between the auditory and word-processing functions, and issues with concentration, which is when learning difficulties may take hold.

Time spent out of the classroom, either through a reluctance to attend school, or imposed exclusion, will further exacerbate the problem. As a child slips behind academically, their anxiety levels will increase, and the cycle continues.

In an educational setting expect to see:

Dramatic/aggressive outbursts

When already operating at a state of high arousal, it does not take very much for a child to become triggered by a seemingly small incident – a word, a look or an accidental shove. Powerful feelings as levels of arousal increase, tend to negatively influence behaviour.

In a classroom situation, a dramatic outburst in response to an apparently minor event may result in a forceful, negative response from the teacher, which pushes an already simmering situation into one that boils over, as a child's fight or flight mode is triggered. A child's emotional outburst may trigger the member of staff in turn, which will often result in further escalation.

It takes time to stop, listen and try to understand another human being, but it is this process that will ultimately bring about positive change.

Dissociation

When children are traumatised, they feel unsafe in the world, and may be unable to connect with the emotions and feelings within their inner selves. Dissociation or 'zoning out' is one of the ways the brain and body cope with high levels of potentially toxic stress hormones for overly long periods.

The difficulty, is that this approach can be perceived by others as an act of defiance, or non-compliance, as a child appears unresponsive to requests from adults, creating further tension.

It is important to be aware that 'zoning out' may in fact be a successful survival strategy for a child who has previously learnt to switch off, and wait for a terrifying or painful episode to conclude. Dissociation may help a child to escape from uncomfortable feelings and physical sensations, in order to calm themselves, a self-soothing strategy. It is extremely unlikely that shouting at a child to focus and concentrate on the task at hand will have the desired outcome.

Regression

A child might behave like a much younger person, or even a baby. This type of reaction needs to be handled sensitively, and with the desire to really understand the behaviour, until a child is ready to move on. There may be all sorts of reasons for a child to act this way. It may be that they remember being cuddled and feeling safe, and want to experience this again. A child might be craving adult attention, and be aware that younger siblings appear to attract greater responsiveness by default. It could be that temporary regression to their younger selves is a way of simplifying things when they don't know what to say or do. It might also indicate an expression of trust in a carer that a child feels safe enough to seek out physical contact and kindness from them.

Numbing

When I hear a child rattle off a list of traumatic personal experiences, one after the other, without apparent emotion or connection to the events, I am both curious and concerned. Why is there an apparent dissociation from the personal narrative? Has the child 'learnt' a succinct version of events to act as a shield, deflecting any shocked or uncomfortable responses before they are uttered? Is the child affected by a fear of rejection, or an inability to physically hear the truth out loud, because of overwhelming feelings of shame? It may also be the case that a child seems preoccupied with something trivial, having almost anaesthetised themselves to the more shocking reality. Be curious.

How does Thera-Build try to reduce the harmful effects of trauma?

Thera-Build provides support for those children who need a little extra help processing their traumatic memories and exploring their feelings and reactions.

Thera-Build relies on the physical manipulation of LEGO® bricks to bring about self-regulation in a secure, supportive, therapeutic environment, where trust, empathy and understanding can calm stress levels, and bring about positive changes in behaviour.

- The Thera-Build programme provides a safe space where children can relax.

- Offers a secure base from which children can trial solutions, approaches and strategies.

- Provides the time a child needs to feel seen and heard.

- Sets clear and consistent boundaries within a playful, nurturing environment.

- Helps children identify, understand and deal with their emotions.

- Explores positive self-regulating activities, to build confidence and resilience.

- Supports children's language and communication skills.

- Nurtures congruent relationships.

- Encourages other adults to notice, understand and try to describe the child's experience.

What is attachment?

Attachment is the connection between a child and their primary care-giver. The type of attachments formed in early life can affect how a child will relate to other people right through into adulthood.

Attachment theory

Attachment theory is the joint work of John Bowlby and Mary Ainsworth, and is a framework for understanding the nature of the bonds that develop between children and their parents – their attachment figures. The theory focuses mainly on relationships during early childhood, and the impact that these have on the emotional development and mental health of children as they grow up. The first three years of a child's life are critical, as it is during this period that the primary attachment bond is set.

Attachment and Thera-Build

The importance of attachment theory in Thera-Build is two-fold. Firstly, attachment relationships play a key role in a child's development, particularly in their concept of 'self', and their perception of others. It is therefore fundamental that Thera-Build practitioners work in an 'attachment aware' way, because understanding a child's attachment style helps a practitioner to work more effectively with a young person.

Secondly, if a child has had confusing or inconsistent responses from their main attachment figure, their behaviour is likely to reflect this. Thera-Build practitioners need to support children to feel secure, to assist and encourage them to manage their own emotions, and to be in charge of their thoughts and behaviours, in order to respond appropriately in situations.

A child's attachments may alter with a change in circumstances, and a child may have a different type of attachment to other family members. Whatever the individual attachment style, it is evident that the more an individual can resolve any trauma from their own childhood, the more capable they will be of forming future healthy adult relationships and a secure attachment with their own child(ren).

Attachment disorder

Attachment-disordered children may well demonstrate rudeness, hostility, defiance and controlling behaviours. They might also present as very helpful, overly compliant and needy of your time and attention, or perhaps appear daydreamy, even absent.

We need to be mindful of and curious about why children behave the way they do, and try to understand these behaviours, taking into consideration their early life history. If a child has experienced a chaotic home life, or suffered neglect or trauma at the hands of the adults who should be their primary care-givers, then pathways in the brain have been laid down that adults are not safe and are not to be relied upon, and a child's behaviour will reflect this.

As we know that a secure attachment provides resilience, regulates the nervous system and underpins general health and well-being, we have to try to meet the unmet needs of those children that, through no fault of their own, developed amidst a backdrop of chaos, fear or neglect.

Thera-Build is rich in positive, healthy experiences for a child. This valuable experience needs to be held in the brain long enough to begin to challenge the brain's default of anxiety, negativity and pessimism, and requires repetition in order for a child to heal.

The four main attachment styles

When we measure attachment, we are essentially measuring self-control and a child's ability to emotionally regulate. This presents as a spectrum of behaviour, from passive right through to hyper-activity – all stemming from poor attachment in the early years.

Attachment style	Likely behaviours	Likely view of adults
Secure (integrated)	Confident, positive, secure, buoyant, asks for help, easily soothed when upset, self-assured and optimistic	Trustworthy, reliable, sensitive, consistent, attuned to child's communications, will meet child's needs
Insecure (anxious)	Clingy, dependent behaviour, especially needy of attention, but may be ambivalent and reject interaction. Feelings of security not internalised, demonstrates separation anxiety, difficulty being calmed and in self-soothing	May offer child some security, but it is patchy and inconsistent and cannot be relied upon. Adults are unable to provide sufficient safety and reassurance. The world is unsafe

cont.

Attachment style	Likely behaviours	Likely view of adults
Insecure (avoidant)	Pseudo-independence and self-sufficiency, likely to reject or avoid comforting because it is too uncomfortable, rely solely on themselves to meet their own needs	Insensitive, unavailable, unresponsive, unpredictable, cannot be relied upon to meet child's needs
Disorganised (needing integration)	Poor social skills, struggles to emotionally regulate, difficulty forming/sustaining relationships, problems managing stress, may dissociate, may be hostile and aggressive. No consistent strategy for comfort-seeking	Unsafe, erratic, untrustworthy, unpredictable, inconsistent. Primary care-giver also primary source of fear, creating insecurity and confusion

Attention needing

The Thera-Build methodology regards 'attention-seeking' behaviour as 'attention needing' – behaviours that are communicating a need. Requiring attention means craving attachment and connection in order to feel safe, a primitive necessity, without which a child is more likely to experience stress and anxiety.

If a child has grown up insecurely attached and is struggling to find suitable attachment figures within the wider family, school or extra-curricular domain, they are more likely to attach to something or someone who is unsuitable. Therefore, children must be provided with repeated opportunities to build quality relationships where they are truly seen, safe, secure and soothed as soon as possible, to strengthen those brain connections. Thera-Build is one such intervention.

How does LEGO® help?

A box of plastic bricks is clearly neither remedy nor cure for children who are struggling socially and emotionally. However, for children who gain pleasure from building with LEGO®, the Thera-Build programme is a useful approach, because it utilises the playful power of LEGO® as a therapeutic device.

LEGO® is not a silver bullet that can erase painful memories, or remove all traces of childhood trauma. Nevertheless, as a valuable, practical tool, alongside a basic therapeutic understanding, LEGO® can be used to build safe, healthy relationships that enable children to engage in helpful, positive dialogue, and to draw out underlying issues that may then be addressed.

Chapter 5

Creating a Secure Alliance with Thera-Build

Children who experience constant uncertainty often live in a state of continual anxiety, as they are overrun by inconsistent responses, unreliable care and are never assured of their own safety and security. This is likely to affect a child's ability to settle and regulate themselves at school, can cause behavioural problems, and make relationships with adults and peers confusing and difficult to negotiate. Communication for children who have experienced early trauma or abuse can be challenging, as they often lack the emotional intelligence to understand their own feelings, and their frustrated attempts to convey their distress to others are often misunderstood.

Behaviour as communication

Thera-Build recognises that behaviour is a communication that needs to be empathically explored. By addressing the causes of the behaviour, rather than merely responding to the fallout, supporting and connecting, rather than punishing and shaming, practitioners can help a child to co-regulate and then to self-regulate, as they begin to make more positive sense of the world.

With large class sizes and the focus heavily on academic attainment in our current education system, it can seem an impossible task for teachers who are trying to instruct, also to be aware of an individual child's behaviour, translate it into its need, keep the child regulated and show empathy. Yet we know that very little learning can be achieved when a child is in a fearful or dysregulated state. This is why pastoral care or external support is often required.

What is a secure alliance?

A secure alliance refers to the felt bond, or connection, between a practitioner and a child: a partnership that aims to provide safety, acceptance and understanding, and to offer pleasure and enable positive change. As Boston-based psychiatrist Bessell van der Kolk points out, 'More than anything else, being able to feel safe with other people defines mental health; safe connections are fundamental to meaningful and satisfying lives' (2014, p.352). The desires for connection and belonging are fundamental, so, the most powerful aspect of the Thera-Build programme is in establishing a secure relationship in which a child feels safe enough to engage, explore and collaborate in the process.

A secure alliance is central to supporting a child's developmental needs, because it is only when a safe relationship is established and down-regulation of the fear response is tackled, that the brain is able to activate new neural pathways. The Thera-Build practitioner is integral to the process, creating safety, by focusing exclusively on the child, being responsive to their cues and using relational listening.

Creating a secure alliance

A secure, therapeutic alliance should be playful, caring, accepting, empathic, congruent and curious, led by a practitioner with the personal qualities and professional skills required to create a safe space.

According to Maslow's 'Hierarchy of Needs' (1943), a child's most basic needs are those of personal survival, followed by the desire for safety and security, before they are able to progress towards 'self-actualization'. By protecting and comforting the children in our care, and helping them to organise their feelings, we can begin to establish firm foundations that can be supported and built upon, so that children can ultimately thrive. The quality of the relationship between the child and practitioner is a very strong predictor of the outcomes of a Thera-Build intervention.

The main building blocks for creating a secure alliance

Environment

Thera-Build should take place in an environment that is physically safe and secure, and psychologically and emotionally supportive, with regular, but flexible routines. The setting plays an important role and should be psychologically informed to create sensory well-being. This means having an awareness of potential triggers such as a colour or smell, that the physical distance between the child and practitioner is comfortable, and ensuring that the arousal level is appropriate. The environment should also be warm, inviting and sufficiently stimulating, enabling children to comfortably engage in playful exploration.

Strong routines and boundaries

All children need to know that they are safe, seen, cared for and valued for who they are, in a secure, predictable environment, with trustworthy and reliable care.

Attachment-disordered children, for whom personal safety is not a given, and who now find it difficult to regulate themselves, have an even greater need to feel accepted and protected, in order to relax and begin to establish trusting relationships.

Practitioners do not need to be rigid or inflexible in their approach, but predictable and consistent.

Transitional objects

Embrace the use of transitional objects as required, into and out of sessions. Children may bring a cuddly toy with them, a favourite Minifigure, their own LEGO® model from home, a book, etc. Use the object to generate conversation and include it where possible.

Unconditional positive regard

This is a term attributed to American psychologist Carl Rogers, and refers to accepting and supporting another person exactly as they are, without judgement, and creating an atmosphere that allows for their healthy development. Thera-Build practitioners need to accept children as they are, so that they can begin to feel understood, safe to communicate freely and honestly, and can begin to let down their defences. Unconditional positive regard means just that; so, Thera-Build should not be withdrawn if the child does something wrong, makes a mistake or does not conform to expectations.

Consistency and congruence

Be genuine, sincere, honest and approachable, demonstrating kindness, compassion and understanding towards young people. Children in crisis will have learnt that adults cannot be trusted or relied upon, and that the world is not a safe place. Thera-Build practitioners should try to counteract these negative life experiences by modelling a healthy, positive and optimistic example.

Attunement

Attunement is the feeling of being in harmony with another. It is vital that Thera-Build practitioners attune to the rhythm and pace of each child initially, and match their arousal strength and energy levels. In practice, this means that if a child bounces into the room loudly, the practitioner should match their energy levels and rhythm of speech and greet the child in a lively manner. If a child is acutely awkward and shy upon arrival, a quieter, gentler acknowledgement would be more appropriate.

Tune into a child's feelings and reflect them back. 'I can feel that. I'm not sure I can make it any easier.' 'I can see that's really difficult right now. Where do you feel it?' Once the practitioner has connected with the child, they can move on to the process of helping the child to co-regulate, by looking for ways to invigorate a lethargic child, or to calm and settle an overexcited child.

Containment

In order to create a safe, therapeutic alliance, the Thera-Build practitioner must have the ability to regulate their own emotional responses, whilst simultaneously supporting a child to co-regulate. This requires self-awareness and the ability to remain separate, whilst showing compassion and empathy.

Playfulness

Anxiety and fear cripple, if not destroy, a child's playful ability; thus, providing safety and security through Thera-Build is vital. Aim to create an atmosphere of joy, enthusiasm, laughter and delight!

Vigilance is required, however, as sometimes the excitement and thrill of a particular building activity, and/or the strengthening of powerful feelings towards the Thera-Build practitioner themselves, can be overwhelming for a child. There is a danger that they might feel so stimulated and confused by the emotions they experience, that they will need help to manage these feelings and bring about self-regulation. This might manifest itself physically in hugs or full-blown body-slams, biting or sitting really close to you; emotionally, as changes in voice pitch, or eyes glazing over; and verbally, when a child expresses, 'I wish you were my X' (usually teacher or parent).

When trust is established and children feel safe to talk about their experiences, thoughts and feelings, the connection is tangible: it can be physically felt. It establishes a warm, secure relationship where a child values themselves, the practitioner and the bond between them.

Humour

When it feels safe and appropriate, comedy can be a suitable device for exploring feelings and behaviours. As a Thera-Build practitioner is not a teacher, from social services or a parent, but becoming a trusted adult, a little playful surprise at small disclosures can be a safe way to explore the potential of underlying shame. It also gives a child the confidence to speak honestly and openly, knowing that the practitioner is not responsible for punishment and does not stand in judgement, but will help the child to explore their behaviour and try to understand it. When both spontaneously laugh, it is often an indication that there is an emerging bond of safety and trust.

Positive touch

Healthy, emotional development requires safe touch. For some children, the power of positive touch can really help them to connect, calm, alleviate anxiety and heal. A hug, for instance, is known to produce oxytocin and serotonin, the 'feel good' chemicals in the brain. Using touch for reassurance, comfort or congratulation, in the form of hand holding, a pat on the back or an arm around a child's shoulders as part of a healthy, therapeutic relationship, can heighten concentration, bolster confidence and enhance self-esteem.

On a more advisory note, touch within a therapeutic alliance must be used with vigilance and care; ensuring that it has been absorbed safely and accepted comfortably by a child before repeating. For those children who missed out on the developmental milestones that involve positive physical connection to soothe, reduce levels of arousal and help them to feel safe, calm and protected, human touch can feel awkward, even physically painful. Use with caution.

Mirroring

Mirroring is a valuable technique for helping a child to build positive relationships, by activating the mirror neurons in the brain. The synchronicity of movement establishes sensitivity, awareness of and connection to another, and presents the early building blocks for teaching empathy. Truly perceiving a child deeply, being attuned to their emotional state, and using facial expressions and body language to convey feelings and reactions, helps a child to learn empathy and improve their social skills.

Get down on the floor and mirror the movements of the child; engage, respond and delight in what is actually happening, rather than forcing a planned agenda. Allow the child to adopt a comfortable position, for example, sitting at a table, lying on the floor, leaning on a cushion, and align yourself in a similar way. Participate in rhythmic, synchronised building movement to create a calm connection, and hear what a child is communicating both verbally and non-verbally.

Empathy

Empathy is perhaps most simply defined as the power of feeling with another. This does not necessitate having had the exact, same life experience, but possessing the ability to sensitively tap into the feelings of another, by connecting with something within that knows that feeling and by staying out of judgement. Empathy involves good communication skills, particularly in relational listening, and requires sensitivity and respect of others' personal worlds.

Children have an innate capacity to experience empathy, but this does not develop on its own. The more opportunities that a child has to experience empathy, the greater their self-awareness and their mindfulness of others should become. Children need an empathic environment around them and for adults to be congruent, understanding and patient, to help the child develop empathy.

Trust

The very first contact with a child is crucial when establishing a therapeutic relationship. Surprisingly, it takes just a tenth of a second to form an impression of a complete stranger based on their appearance, and those judgements play a powerful role in how a person will go on to treat others. A genuine smile, and sitting on the floor with the LEGO® at the first meeting, usually encourages a positive split-second impression, and an eagerness to play.

When children appear happy and motivated during a session, it is safe to assume that a playful alliance has begun. However, building trust takes time, and an hour a week for six weeks can be a challenging time frame, particularly for looked-after children.

Keep a child within their 'window of tolerance'

The 'window of tolerance' is the level of arousal at which a child functions most successfully, which will, of course, be unique to the individual. In this state, a child will be able to respond appropriately to home or school demands, without feeling either inhibited or overwhelmed.

If a child is nudged out of their window of tolerance by too much stress, the prefrontal cortex of the brain begins to shut down, and this is when we can expect to see examples of either hyper or hypo arousal (fight, flight, freeze).

Keeping a child within their personal window of tolerance through a secure, therapeutic relationship, supporting them to understand the physical sensations that might suggest an oncoming change of state and teaching children techniques to remain within their window of tolerance, calming and soothing themselves to manage their arousal level, all help to prevent dysregulation.

Breathing

Learning how to breathe, in order to train the arousal system, is another helpful part of the Thera-Build programme. When a child is distressed from an incident that has just occurred, or is remembering a painful experience, ask them to 'stop and take a breath' initially, then encourage them to relax by steady, deep breathing exercises, if required.

The simple act of letting a child have a few minutes of peace alone, under a blanket or school jumper, knowing that you are on hand and that they are in a safe space, can help to bring their breathing back into check, and aid emotional regulation.

Music designed for relaxation or a mindful story may prove beneficial. Bubble blowing, windmills, glitter bottles or party blowers may be helpful aids to calm breathing and the nervous system too (see Chapter 10).

A successful secure alliance

Essentially a secure therapeutic alliance is the reliable and comforting relationship that is built between a child and practitioner, which relies upon trust, and allows for an effective, positive bond to develop, in which a child feels seen, safe, secure and soothed.

Children need to know that you are interested in them, feel that you care about them and believe that you have their best interests at heart.

• Chapter 6 •

Using LEGO® to Self-Regulate and Self-Soothe

Within a secure therapeutic alliance, Thera-Build practitioners help children to understand where their behaviours come from, introduce positive strategies for self-soothing and guide children towards independent self-regulation. Thera-Build teaches a little about brain integration, and provides playful, practical activities to bring the left- and right-brain hemispheres, which may have become wildly out of balance, back into equilibrium.

If a child does not like building with LEGO®, then please don't use it, because it will not help a child to calm down, or result in self-regulation. In fact, the irritation, unpleasant sensory experience and building frustration experienced by a 'LEGO® refuser' will, in all probability, have the opposite effect!

The therapeutic methodology behind Thera-Build still remains relevant, but a different medium such as modelling clay, painting, collage, puppetry or sand play will be of greater restorative value.

What is self-regulation?

Self-regulation is the ability to manage personal emotional responses, thoughts and behaviours in any given situation, and is necessary for emotional well-being. In reality this means being able to control impulsive and inappropriate behaviour, so that verbal outbursts, emotional meltdowns and temper tantrums are contained, to handle frustration, adapt to change and be able to calm those automatic primal reactions when upset.

Learning to co-regulate

Attachment theory promotes the view that a reliable and responsive primary care-giver who is attuned to an infant's needs is the most effective means by which a young child learns to emotionally regulate. Children who have not experienced a secure attachment in their early years, and whose basic developmental needs were not met, may struggle to regulate their emotions, and find themselves getting into challenging cycles of behaviour at home and at school, with other children and adults.

Learning the skills to self-regulate and self-soothe is not something that comes naturally, or instinctively, to children who have developed amidst a setting of trauma or neglect. The ability to regulate oneself is not possible without a child first experiencing a basic level of safety, and is made even more problematic if a child lacks the familiarity to know what calmness and composure actually feel like for themselves. We must provide the support and guidance that was so lacking in their formative years, to help such children first learn the basics of co-regulation, to understand that emotional pain and suffering can be healed with the support of a trusted aide, and that there are successful practical strategies that can be adopted to alleviate the pain of fear and abandonment, through playful, healthy, building experiences, in which children can safely connect with another.

If circumstances allow, it is hugely beneficial to observe a child *in situ*, without intervening, to monitor their experiences. A detailed observation should take approximately fifteen minutes per session, the child should be unaware that they are the focal point, and the practitioner should record everything that they witness involving the child, within that short time frame. A Thera-Build observation sheet is included in the Appendix. Observing a child closely and objectively is one of many sources of information that may be gathered to determine a child's needs, prior to the start of a Thera-Build intervention.

Prioritise the identified needs so that the focus is not too broad, and concentrate on working together in playful building activity, to help the child to regulate with support. Bear in mind that the window of opportunity for self-regulation is very small before emotions become unmanageable. So, where possible, stay with a child at potential trigger points, to help them manage their emotions and assist them in bringing the left- and right-brain hemispheres into balance. This co-regulation is hugely beneficial and necessary, as a precursor to helping a child to self-soothe.

Supporting regulation

- *NOTICE* when a child is starting to become dysregulated. *Voice changes, flinching, humming, agitation, etc.*

- Be *CURIOUS* about the triggers/behaviours. *Has something happened? Does the child feel unsafe?*

- *SUPPORT* the child to understand what is happening internally. *You seem... You look... I noticed that... I think you might...*

- *MODEL* how to respond positively. *Be supportive, empathic, accepting, encouraging and congruent.*

- *HELP* to recover and restore their energy. *Provide practical soothing strategies or playful activities to engage in together.*

How to tell when a child is becoming anxious or dysregulated

Children become dysregulated due to a loss of brain integration. Their behaviour may become confused or chaotic, aggressive and challenging, or result in a complete meltdown, as a child becomes overwhelmed by their emotions.

Some early signs of anxiety or disintegration are:

- changes to voice tone, pitch or speed

- becoming tense or rigid, flinching or jumping

- changes in skintone or temperature, tears in their eyes

- looking startled or zoning out (daydreaming)

- becoming increasingly active, for example, rocking, fiddling with things, being silly

- telling stories, humming or singing inappropriately.

Learning to self-regulate

Never in the entire history of calming down, has anyone ever calmed down by being told to!

Anon.

All children (and some adults!) would benefit from learning self-regulating techniques so that they can begin to understand, and then manage their emotions. Remarkably, many people who are unable to regulate their emotional state are also unaware that they have the power to change it. The most effective way to bring about brain balance and restore calm is to initially validate a person's feelings by connecting to their right brain. Ignoring, shouting over or misunderstanding a child when their right brain is in control will probably cause an escalation of emotions and in behaviour.

Some useful questions/comments might be:

'I can see how upset you are. Would you like to go down to the LEGO® Room, or are you okay sitting quietly with me for a while?'

'Hmmm, it sounds to me like you are feeling X.'

'Let's just stop, and take a breath.'

'You feel X, is that right?'

'I can see that's really difficult right now. Where do you feel it?'

'I can tell this really upsets you.'

'I can feel that. I'm not sure I can make it any easier.'

'Tell me how you feel. I want to help.'

If we accept that fear, anger and anxiety can disrupt the ability to reason and respond consciously, then it is of vital importance that we first address a child's sense of safety, before we help them to understand their behaviours and reactions. That is not to say that they should be exempt from experiencing the consequences of their actions, but suggests a time of appropriate pause and reflection before any disciplinary action is taken. It may well be that a child is repeating a pattern of behaviour that helped to protect them from danger in the past, which would be a perfectly reasonable response. So, be curious about a child's behaviour and the circumstances that led up to an incident, to try to understand it from the child's point of view. Only then can the behaviour be better understood and addressed, so that a child can be presented with alternative solutions for tackling their issues.

Practical strategies

We cannot change or eradicate what has happened to a child in their past, but we can support them to adapt and feel more comfortable with the people around them, give them the safety of consistent routine and provide an accessible, empathic and comforting ear in the present. This does require time, patience and some experimentation, as we are dealing with individual personalities in unique positions, but in this state a child doesn't know *how* to calm themselves, so we have to help them with the process, and empower them to take control of their feelings and understand their own internal world.

- Use anchoring exercises so that a child can check and change their arousal levels.

- Listen to what children have to say, observe and be curious about their behaviours.

- Connect emotionally to a child's right brain initially, then bring it into balance with the left.

- Provide opportunities for a child to experience what it is to feel calm and peaceful.

- Help a child learn the difference between sensations and feelings and be able to label them.

- Break tasks down into manageable time periods.

- As children learn to concentrate and take more control, stretch their window of tolerance.

- Model ways of talking about feelings and emotions, and encourage children to ask for help and support when managing their behaviour.

- Teach children about their internal system, giving them the skills to measure their emotions.

- Provide manageable challenges to promote healthy emotional regulation.

- Scaffold positive responses, offer new vocabulary and state expectations calmly and consistently.

- Coach children by encouraging positive behaviour, until they can manage independently.

- Help children stop and take a breath, to prevent impulsivity.

- Tune into the child's feelings and reflect them back.

- Explore effective responses via the cognitive behavioural therapy (CBT) model.

Useful Thera-Build activities are included in Chapter 10 for further exploration.

What to avoid

A zero-tolerance policy. This doesn't address the roots of the problem and will have little effect, as the 'learning brain' is no longer online and the 'survival brain' is in charge. At this point threatening a sanction if a child doesn't calm down to order will just add to their stress – and yours!

Time-out as punishment. Whilst it may be necessary to temporarily remove a child from a situation, this should be an opportunity for them to rest, regulate and restore, rather than being relegated to a 'sin-bin' or detained in solitary confinement as a punishment.

Withdrawal of Thera-Build for 'bad' behaviour. It might seem that session removal is a very attractive bargaining chip to force conformity, but the traumatised child is not purposefully setting out to get into trouble. Thera-Build should therefore not be used as a reward or prize, but as a much-needed intervention for children who have missed out on vital developmental milestones.

Report cards/behaviour charts. These offer little value, and are particularly unhelpful for children who have experienced trauma. Being continuously observed, assessed and judged is unnecessary pressure to place on a child, rather unimaginative and is likely to fail, as the child's actual needs are not being recognised. 'The capacity of the prefrontal cortex to play a rational, inhibitory role – for example, by weighing the value of an immediate reward against a long-term gain or cost – is significantly reduced when someone's stress load is excessive' (Shanker and Barker 2017, p.14).

Improve communication skills

Without sufficient language skills or emotional intelligence to recognise and articulate how they are feeling, a child may be limited to an angry outburst, or sudden urge to escape. When a child lacks the vocabulary and skill to understand their internal condition, they may be limited to simple responses, 'I am angry' or 'I feel sad', and, coupled with a determination to keep themselves safe by staying in control, will avoid anybody, or any situation, that makes them feel uncomfortable or challenged.

Hiding from, or lacking awareness of, true core feelings can really eat away at a person's sense of self, and be very confusing for a child. Aggressive behaviour may be a means of temporarily masking the primary emotion and releasing some of the fear or terror residing within. On the other hand, for some children an acknowledgement that 'I am angry' might be a really sophisticated response, especially for a child who experienced trauma prior to language development, so there are no hard and fast rules that can be applied.

Children who live daily with uncertainty, brutality or cynicism may well be confused by, or suspicious of, anybody treating them kindly. When being rude, aggressive or hurtful is the norm, compliments or compassion may well prove perplexing and a child might be unsure about how to respond. For the same reasons eye contact or positive touch should be used with care.

Helping children to tell their story, explain their truth, however painful, and to communicate fully with a Thera-Build practitioner may provide them with a fresh perspective. By sharing their confusion, terror and hurt with another, the hope is that a child can reconnect positively and healthily with other human beings.

Is a child's age important?

Whilst awareness of a child's chronological age is important in terms of presenting appropriate bricks and themes, particular consideration must also be given to the assessment of a child's emotional age.

Children who have missed out on a secure early attachment, and whose brain development has subsequently been hindered, may find it more difficult to process things in line with age-related expectations, finding it more challenging to play safely and to learn. It is far more beneficial to offer a free-building activity, or to start with a simple building project using fewer, or larger bricks, to boost confidence and self-esteem, than to introduce a build that is too challenging.

> **Case Example**: Chelsea, aged 10, had bolted out of class, barricaded herself into the school nurture room and was refusing to come out. She had moved furniture up against the door and covered the glass, so that nobody could see inside. I had an appointment with the head teacher that day to discuss the use of Thera-Build as a possible intervention

for the school to adopt, and our meeting was interrupted by this incident.

After a few minutes of gentle, reassuring conversation from the head teacher and an introduction through a closed door, two anxious eyes peeped out and I was granted admission to the room. Chelsea looked extremely tired, so we both propped ourselves up on beanbags and used conversation to begin to build the foundations of a secure alliance.

I had no LEGO® with me, so asked Chelsea to tell me about the room that we were in and the resources it contained. There were several books on a shelf and I offered to read her a story, an invitation that was readily accepted. There was a dog in the story and afterwards we talked about pets, then Chelsea did an impression of a puppy and we delved into some imaginative play as I mirrored her, attuning and responding to her need for safety.

After a while Chelsea asked me if I would like to get out the Play-Doh®, which we did. Her artistic talents were clear for anyone to see, in terms of mark-making and modelling, which started a dialogue about her absent, artist father and a lengthy description of the sorts of art activities she most enjoys. We discovered a small box of LEGO® in the room, and combined the two materials, by rolling out pizza bases from the Play-Doh and decorating them with LEGO® elements to represent various toppings.

This evolved into further role-play as Chelsea became the pizza chef and I was the customer, ordering a variety of pizzas for a party. We pretended to be different people in the pizzeria, making up stories and laughing at each other's silly voices or hideous pizza combinations.

When the head teacher returned, Chelsea's brain was back in balance, she was more comfortable, relaxed and able to reconnect. She briefly talked through the incident with the head teacher and, although she was unable to explain or understand her behaviour at that stage, she was receptive to a healthy dialogue about the incident, before returning to class.

This initial play bond was reminiscent of my time in Nursery, rather than Year 5, but it was what *Chelsea* needed there and then. For those who perceive Thera-Build as a 'reward for bad behaviour' I would respectfully suggest that schools are already working with children who are demonstrating challenging behaviours as a result of their early development, and that if something as simple as play and connection can help towards healing these children, then it would be foolish to ignore, dismiss or indeed condemn Thera-Build as a positive intervention, just because children enjoy it.

Thera-Build to further emotional development

It is important to recognise the foundation that emotional development establishes for later growth and development in children. A child's emotional needs might affect their social interactions, have a bearing on their behaviour, influence their decision-making and impact their ability to be receptive to learning, and should therefore receive the same consideration as other areas of development.

Thera-Build encourages and supports children to:

- actively identify and understand their true feelings
- manage powerful emotions and express them appropriately
- develop empathy for others
- establish and maintain positive relationships.

The success of a child's emotional development is very dependent on:

- their individual personal experiences
- influences of the environments in which they live
- the quality of their social interactions.

Chapter 7

Meeting Developmental Needs and Listening Skills

Sense of self

How young children view themselves has a direct link to their success as learners. Their self-identity is strongly influenced by their surroundings, and the way they are treated by the people around them. They will pick up on visual, verbal and non-verbal clues, to determine how well they are liked and accepted by others. Thera-Build aims to help children to develop a healthy, positive and realistic sense of identity.

Self-esteem

High self-esteem	Low self-esteem
• Willingly attempts new tasks and challenges • Performs confidently and independently • Takes pride in accomplishments • Assumes responsibility • Tolerates frustration • Handles positive and negative emotions • Offers assistance to others	• Avoids trying new things • Feels unloved, unwanted and useless • Puts down own talents and abilities • Blames others when weakens or fails • Unable to tolerate an ordinary level of frustration • Struggles to emotionally regulate • Is easily influenced by others

Meeting specific developmental needs with LEGO®

There are a number of developmental needs that all children have in order to develop into healthy adults. If these needs are not met as children, it may deeply impact a child's sense of self, and young people will continue to try to have these needs met right into adulthood and beyond. This clearly has significant implications for the next generation, as children mature, and become parents themselves.

Remember that children and young people need to be empathically *seen*, kept *safe* and *secure*, and be *soothed* by their care providers, as we tend to their developmental needs.

The developmental need for belonging/connection

Children need to feel that they belong to a group or family, and will always try to find a place where they fit in. Not feeling that they belong anywhere can lead to emotional, even physical death.

Thera-Build suggested activities:

- Build with LEGO® together. This may be in a one-to-one intervention, involve a small group of peers or could involve the whole family in a theme or project.

- Play LEGO® board games together.

- Work on a problem-solving challenge together.

- Start a group building project that can be added to over days, weeks or even months.

The developmental need for mirroring

Children need to be seen, heard and praised. When not mirrored the child feels shame, and if consistently not mirrored, the child may not even try to make any further contact.

Thera-Build suggested activities:

- Be physically close to a child as they play, rhythmically building together.

- Comment positively on the choice of bricks used, or the model coming to life.

- Praise children for their resourcefulness, innovation, creativity, ability to concentrate, teamwork, etc.

- Actively listen, using comfortable eye contact and positive touch.

The developmental need for merger

Children need to feel as if they are part of another, deeply connected, safe and soothed. When a child has not had this developmental need met, they have a general feeling of not being safe.

Thera-Build suggested activities:

- Focus specifically on creating a strong, secure alliance as you build together.

- Sit closely together whilst building, so that you attune to each other.

- Synchronise with the child's breathing pattern and help to regulate their breath.

- Remember previous conversations to draw upon, further develop and explore.

The developmental need for twinship

Children need to do things with, or copy adults. When this need is not met, children learn that they don't have value. As a result, they may be constantly wanting attention and connection.

Thera-Build suggested activities:

- Give children your time. Join in with LEGO® building, or take an interest in their models.

- Build together, or assist a child, by organising the bricks and finding the correct elements.

- Encourage children to explore and develop their own interests with LEGO®, for example, space, by providing opportunities to work together on projects such as constructing a space station or building a LEGO® orrery.

- Model positive behaviour, healthy dialogue and optimistic outcomes.

The developmental need for initiating

Children need to be shown *how* to do things. They also need to know that what they are feeling is seen and understood by another. Unrealistic expectations of a child's ability will have a negative effect on confidence and self-esteem, which may make them less likely to try out new things, and more likely to deliberately spoil their models.

Thera-Build suggested activities:

- Choose a manageable but challenging building project that you can work on collaboratively.

- Pair up as 'builder' and 'supplier' to team-build towards a specific goal, following the LEGO® building instructions, and ensure that you swap roles regularly.

- Notice if a child gets stuck on a particular part of modelling, such as roof-building, and offer to show them some options for problem-solving a solution.

- Explore online tutorials, building instructions and videos to learn from, discuss or reproduce.

Crucial requirements for children and young people

- *Time* to play and build alongside each other, or together if invited.

- *Encouragement* to explore and develop their own interests with LEGO®, for example insects or vehicles.

- *Praise* for their resourcefulness, innovation, creativity, concentration, teamwork, etc.

- *Assistance* if they get stuck on a particular construction issue, such as adding wheels.

- Positive touch and eye contact where appropriate.

- Constructive comments on the choice of bricks used, or the model coming to life.

- Opportunities to converse together, paying particular attention to listening.

Listening skills

Quality listening is of paramount importance when building alongside a child in a Thera-Build session. Listening is not about being silent, waiting for a child to finish their sentence, in order to provide a verbal response. It involves being present with a child, mindfully listening in the moment to what is being said, noticing how it is being said, observing and being a part of the construction activity, and listening to the play narrative that arises as a result. Practitioners must allow time for the process of speaking and listening to evolve naturally, and not rush it forward to suit their targets, provide solutions or to make judgements. Listen empathically, because it is the bond that you are creating, rather than a verbal response that will be most comforting and helpful to a child.

When a child invites a practitioner into their construction or imaginative play, it is a privilege. Listen to what it is the child would like you to do. Do they want you to play a particular character, to move their story or game along, or are they asking for your assistance because they literally need a hand to join two elements together? Listen, so that you can respond appropriately to their needs. By all means make suggestions, but guard against taking over the activity, or conversation. Thera-Build practitioners should facilitate the process and allow children the power to make their own play choices, as long as they are safe.

In reality, there are times when a practitioner may lose focus: they may feel weary, or be distracted by another imminent task requiring their attention. It is imperative to fully focus on the child, the building activity at hand and the enjoyment of the play experience, because a child will be rapidly alerted to an adult tuning out, and this will affect their sense of self and the therapeutic relationship.

Avoiding subject areas

Give sorrow words; the grief that does not speak.
Whispers the o'er-fraught heart and bids it break.

William Shakespeare, *Macbeth*

Whilst building together, children will often talk openly about their experiences, and it is our job as practitioners to listen, empathise and try to help them make sense of often very difficult events. We should not sugarcoat a situation, but listen and be honest in our responses, perhaps exploring different possibilities or perspectives where appropriate. If a child brings up a topic, I will not avoid it. If they feel safe enough to ask about something, then we do just that. Talking may prove upsetting, but is unlikely to make matters worse.

Case Example: Jake, aged 11, was often in trouble at school, for being angry and aggressive, with staff and pupils alike, and was prone to frequent absences from school. When he was 9, Jake's mother was diagnosed with cancer and, as the family prepared for the worst, his father was killed right in front of him in a bicycle accident. Jake was living with his mum, for whom medical treatment seemed to be successfully working, and his elder brother when I first met him.

In our Thera-Build sessions I found Jake to be a considerate, quiet, compliant young man, who was very calm and gentle. He was extremely helpful in organising the new LEGO® that the school had sourced, and enjoyed rhythmically sorting through and ordering the bricks into the storage trays with me. He didn't speak very much initially, and so our conversations tended to be about the LEGO® we were building with, or the particular theme or activity we were involved in, during each session.

Gradually, as Jake began to talk more about his own circumstances, illness became a reccurring theme, and it also became obvious that loud noises, particularly shouting, 'make me feel mad'. Jake struggled to make decisions when given a choice, frequently stating, 'I am happy with whatever you choose', and displayed poor construction skills and spatial confusion, so needed a lot of building support.

Over time as our connection strengthened, Jake began to volunteer fragments of information about his personal life: 'When my mum had cancer, all her hair fell out.' I did not shy away from the conversation because Jake had instigated it. Physically having the LEGO® between us was really beneficial, as we were generally facing one another on the floor, and it meant that we could build whilst conversing, casually averting our eyes to the bricks, which lessened the intensity of the discussion. I pushed no agenda other than to ensure that Jake felt seen, safe and secure and was enjoying our time together. In point of fact, both his fine and gross motor skills came on in leaps and bounds as a result of the focused building time.

I used to see Jake weekly, and it took several months for him even to mention his dad. On one particular day, there was a LEGO® bicycle amongst the elements, which Jake selected, and asked, 'Did you know that my dad died?' We had a brief conversation surrounding the basic facts, and the initial aftermath, and then continued to play.

The following week Jake asked if we could build a skatepark together. We assembled a textured surface with ramps and other obstacles on the baseplate, and then he built Minifigures that he mounted on LEGO® skateboards, scooters and bikes, and flipped them around doing stunts on the scenery. He had them pulling 'wheelies', which is what his father was doing when he fell back and hit his head, and this seemed to unlock something within. Jake felt safe and ready to explore the horror he had witnessed at his own pace, and in his own way, with a trusted adult to guide and support him.

For children who experienced considerable levels of trauma as young babies, and were therefore pre-verbal, it is extremely hard for them to go about making sense of their memories. We know that avoidance of the feelings associated with these recollections only increases the likelihood of being overwhelmed by them, so however difficult or unbearable the sensations are, we should try to tackle them.

It is not important to tease out all of the details from a traumatic event, but to support the child to tolerate their feelings and consider healthier ways of managing them, so that they feel in charge of their responses and their life choices. Memories are not always precise commentaries, and recall of a traumatic event can be patchy and vague, with small features emerging at a much later date. These can provoke a powerful emotional response and affect a child's level of arousal, so be prepared to respond.

Verbal blocks to listening

When listening to a child, try to avoid:

- judging, moralising and criticising
- use of sarcasm
- referring to yourself
- blaming and using labels
- using logic, or interrupting with your own views or solutions
- asking too many probing questions, particularly through closed questioning
- pointing out discrepancies within a narrative
- minimising, or negating an experience.

Non-verbal blocks to listening

Certain behaviours can be extremely offputting, if not hurtful when employed, giving off such messages as 'You are boring me, this is a waste of my time', 'I do not value you and I am not interested in what you are saying', 'I have other more important things to be doing'. Try to avoid:

- fidgeting, eating, sighing or yawning

- inappropriate or closed facial expressions or body language

- a lack of congruence between expressions and words

- repeatedly checking the time

- not noticing when a prompt is needed

- inappropriate eye contact, be it too much, or too little

- distractions, such as looking out of the window, or fiddling with a pen.

Paraphrasing

Paraphrasing can be a really helpful way to demonstrate under-standing, and to develop trust. By putting a child's thoughts and feelings into their own words, a practitioner is seeking to make connections and to achieve greater clarity. It shows a child that they have been listened to, and also gives them the chance to correct any parts that are ambiguous, or that have been misunderstood. Children need to feel heard and understood.

Chapter 8

Thera-Build and Simple Cognitive Behavioural Therapy

Our life is what our thoughts make it.

Marcus Aurelius, *Meditations*

What is cognitive behavioural therapy (CBT)?

CBT is a short-term psychotherapy treatment, proven to be effective in handling a variety of emotional, psychological and behavioural difficulties. It is a goal-orientated approach that relies on the recipient being actively involved in problem-solving their own issues.

CBT is a practical talking therapy, and its main purpose is to examine, and help people to change the way that they think, or behave, in order to manage their current difficulties. By challenging a person's beliefs and preconceptions of themselves, of others and the world around them, CBT can help people to change the way that they feel.

The therapist provides the tools and teaches the skills to facilitate the process of change, but it requires time and effort on behalf of the beneficiary to achieve the desired outcome(s). If an individual is unwilling, or unable, to learn new skills and to put them into practice, then CBT will not be effective.

Thera-Build and the basic principles of CBT

Thera-Build practitioners are not therapists; however, some of the more basic 'common-sense' principles of CBT theory can be safely applied to a Thera-Build intervention.

CBT explores how thoughts, feelings and behaviours can form a vicious cycle, sometimes referred to as the 'problem maintenance cycle', that can influence and reinforce negative sequences that perpetuate the problem(s).

Practitioners should pay close attention to the relationship between a child's thoughts, feelings and behaviours, to look for unhelpful patterns, or underlying beliefs, that result in problems for that child, and their wider community. When a child interprets an event in a negative way, they might experience negative emotions; those negative feelings could lead on to negative behaviour, which will lead on to further negative thoughts, and so on.

The aim is to examine confused or distorted patterns of thought, to increase a child's self-awareness and to challenge dysfunctional thinking. The practitioner should encourage the young person to question their thoughts, and to find alternative, realistic, more rational explanations, which will increase feelings of well-being, resulting in improved behaviour and raised aspirations.

Thera-Build practitioners work with children towards beneficial change:

- to reduce worry and stress

- to increase self-awareness

- to improve self-control

- to raise confidence and self-esteem, and learn skills to positively assert themselves

- to notice arousal levels and understand that they can be changed

- to identify and challenge unhelpful thoughts

- to tackle negative behaviour cycles

- to appreciate that interactions between thoughts, feelings and behaviours impact each other, whether positive or negative

- to safely examine distressing memories.

The problem maintenance cycle

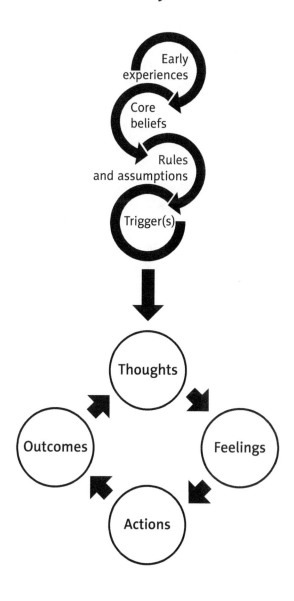

Weaving CBT into Thera-Build

Thera-Build is primarily based around building, playing and talking, and for younger children in particular, any form of writing in the session should be discouraged. It may be helpful at times for an older child to record some written information for later reference.

Useful, practical strategies
Thoughts, feelings and actions activity cards

It can be really difficult for children and young people to specify how they are actually feeling, and they often talk about how they are thinking, or what happened, instead. Try this activity to encourage a child to identify the differences between thoughts, feelings and actions. Cut out the cards and ask the child to position them under the correct headings, and discuss their placement.

Thoughts	Feelings	Actions
I am going to mess this up	Angry	Going to school
This is really wonderful	Sad	Having fun with friends
None of the teachers like me	Disappointed	Shouting
I'm pretty good at art	Frustrated	Grabbing a snack
Nobody cares what I do	Jealous	Watching TV
I am very pleased with myself	Happy	Playing football
I am easy to get along with	Shocked	Crying
I am useless at schoolwork	Anxious	Reading a book

Red and green thoughts

To further develop a child's emotional intelligence, explore both positive and negative thoughts together. Ask the child to identify which are helpful (green) thoughts, and which are unhelpful (red) thoughts.

Provide example cards, and blanks, for children to include their own thoughts for discussion.

Helpful thoughts	Unhelpful thoughts
I give most things a try	Whatever I do, it goes wrong
Things always get better	Something bad is bound to happen
Everyone makes mistakes	I am just not as good as other people

Thoughtful reflections

- Start with a particular event, trigger or situation.

- Discuss helpful and unhelpful thoughts.

- If appropriate, develop this further into associated feelings, behaviours and outcomes.

Example:

Trigger/Event: When I came into the classroom this morning, my friend didn't notice me.	
Helpful thoughts: My friend didn't see me when I arrived My friend behaved unusually. Are they okay?	**Unhelpful thoughts:** My friend ignored me. What did I do? My friend doesn't like me any more
Helpful feelings: I feel comfortable, happy and secure I am concerned about my friend's well-being	**Unhelpful feelings:** A stabbing feeling in my tummy I feel really sad, confused and upset
Helpful behaviours: Go over and check on my friend Find out if I can help my friend with anything	**Unhelpful behaviours:** Say something spiteful to my friend Avoid and ignore my friend all day
Helpful outcomes: We talk and laugh together, like normal We both meet up for lunch later	**Unhelpful outcomes:** I get into a fight with my friend We both get a detention from the teacher

Thought records

Encourage young people to bring some balance to their thought processes by scrutinising a negative thought objectively, in the way that a judge might examine evidence. Is this a helpful thought? If not, dispute it! Is the thought accurate? Reliable? Is there an alternative explanation? What would you say to a friend?

Work with young people to explore their initial thoughts and look for patterns of thinking.

- What was your automatic thought?

- What evidence supports the thought?

- What evidence does not support the thought?

- What would be an alternative or balanced thought?

- What might other people think?

Blank template:

Trigger/Event:	
Helpful thoughts:	Unhelpful thoughts:
Helpful feelings:	Unhelpful feelings:
Helpful behaviours:	Unhelpful behaviours:
Helpful outcomes:	Unhelpful outcomes:

Changing negative reactions and improving outcomes

Help children to understand that when things happen, they have a choice about how to react. The way that they interpret and respond to an event largely determines the impact the trigger has on their mood.

Build a situation that the young person has struggled with, from LEGO®, and discuss it together.

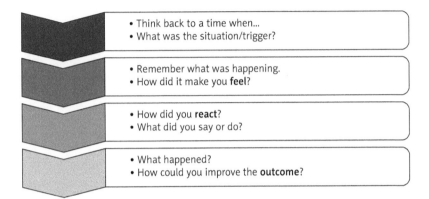

- Think back to a time when...
- What was the situation/trigger?

- Remember what was happening.
- How did it make you **feel**?

- How did you **react**?
- What did you say or do?

- What happened?
- How could you improve the **outcome**?

Explore different responses together to improve outcomes, by focusing on healthy and positive reactions.

It may be really useful to have several baseplates to build multiple scenarios, or simply to modify one baseplate by making positive, physical changes to it.

Taking photographs at different stages of the process can be really helpful.

Exploring feelings

It is important to recognise that as human beings, we:

- experience a range of feelings and emotions

- might encounter several emotions at any one time

- understand that opposing emotions can trigger similar physical responses

- need to recognise, name and understand feelings, in order to manage them.

In order to help children connect to their emotions, some work needs to be done around the physical sensations behind the words. Exploring the bodily feelings that are experienced when various strong emotions are activated, for example, where they are positioned (tummy, head, palms of hands) and describing how they feel (butterflies, pounding drum, sweaty) can be really powerful in helping a child to understand what is going on in their inner world, and what that might mean.

Many children, particularly those who have experienced childhood trauma, have difficulty describing what they are feeling, as they do not understand themselves what is going on internally. When feeling anxious, for instance, an uncomfortable feeling may emerge in the tummy, making a child think that they are hungry. They need to understand what they are feeling, before they can even begin to think about why.

The Thera-Build practitioner may use open questions and prompts to draw out a child's feelings, by asking 'I'm wondering if you are feeling…?', 'What was that like for you?', 'How did you feel when…?', 'Is it possible that you might be feeling…?'

When sufficient work has been done around labelling emotions, ask children to try to explain their mood(s) or that of another, using succinct bursts of 'feelings vocabulary', for example, 'Angry', 'Sad', 'Empty', rather than long, rambling sentences that might confuse thoughts and feelings. Once the feelings have been identified and understood, young people can be helped to manage them.

The construction of 'Mood Monsters' from LEGO® is an excellent activity for examining the physical manifestations of certain emotions, and looking at positive coping strategies. See www.build-happy.co.uk for the resource and upcoming training dates (Thomsen and Green 2016).

Set target goals

When a Thera-Build intervention is first put in place, specified outcomes are documented, but not necessarily shared with the child. In many cases those targets remain the practitioner's focus and are worked towards playfully. For other children, it can be helpful to understand the reasons behind the intervention, and goal-setting provides a helpful framework that they understand and work towards.

Do not overwhelm a child by concentrating on a whole list of targets; just focus on one goal at a time, and keep it very low key.

- Plan with a child what they hope to achieve from an intervention.

- Write down each target.

- Map out a strategy for addressing the goals.

- Make sure that the plan is realistic, specific and manageable.

- Break each stage down into convenient steps.

- Practically work together towards completion.

Brick rotations

A brick rotation is a diagram that can be completed by the young person, or the practitioner, to record and monitor thoughts, feelings and actions. Discuss how changing just one aspect can positively alter outcomes.

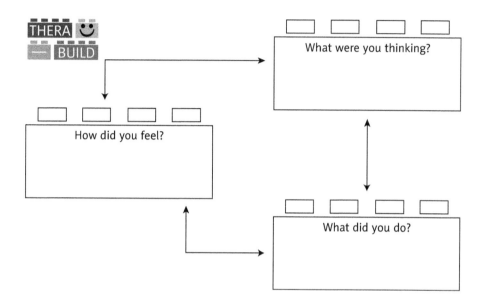

Chapter 9

The Practicalities of Resourcing, Hygiene and Organisation

What age group is Thera-Build designed for?

Thera-Build is most commonly practised with children aged 5–13, but is adaptable to meet the needs of both pre-schoolers and teens.

Thera-Build intervention duration

A Thera-Build intervention programme usually lasts for 6, 12 or 18 sessions, depending upon the individual needs of the child(ren). The initial assessment period occurs within the first 6-week block.

Session length

Each Thera-Build session usually lasts between 45 minutes and 1 hour. Some children might require more time than others to transition in and out of sessions, particularly in a special educational needs and disability (SEND) setting. It is necessary to allow for this when planning, to ensure that a good solid period of at least 30 minutes is spent playing/building.

What group size makes Thera-Build most effective?

Depending on the developmental needs of the group, the targeted outcomes of the intervention process and the environment, working in a ratio of 1:8 is possible. The most common group size, however, would be 1:4 in order to provide the children with sufficient concentrated time, resources and space.

What LEGO® is required to implement Thera-Build?

It would be futile to provide references to a specific kit list, as this would become quickly outdated by the rapid change in the LEGO® product lines. A collection of basic bricks and the imagination to use them creatively is all that is required when starting out; this can be added to as and when budgets allow.

When sourcing a LEGO® collection to deliver Thera-Build, aim to acquire, in this sequence:

- a substantial supply of classic building bricks

- baseplates of various colours and sizes

- a variety of wheels and axles

- a collection of Minifigures

- a number of specialist elements to add detail, such as doors, windows and slope bricks

- a quantity of other accessories to expand play, such as animals, scenery, battlements, rock panels, pulleys and turntables.

Where to source LEGO®

- accept bricks from anyone willing to donate them, sort and clean before use

- car boot sales, second-hand toy sales

- online auction sites or advertising pages

- toy shops, department stores and supermarkets

- 'Pick a Brick' walls at LEGO® Stores, LEGOLAND® or online.

How to store LEGO® models

The storing of LEGO® models will of course be dependent upon individual circumstances and settings. Access to a secure place, such as a locked cupboard onsite is ideal, allowing for models to stay safe, intact and accessible. Peripatetic practitioners should carry a suitably sized container to transit a model for later development.

Always take photographs of a child's model, particularly at the end of a session. These may be instantly printed off for the child to keep, or mounted in a child's 'Building Booklet', which would contain pictures of all their models, and some commentary where appropriate, as an individual record of their Thera-Build journey.

How to keep LEGO® clean

Use a number of preventative measures to keep LEGO® sets clean:

- Do not allow the bricks to be taken outside.

- Do not allow food and drink to be consumed around the bricks.

- Do not leave models in the full glare of UV light, as this fades the bricks.

It is incredible how smelly dust from the floor can be when it infiltrates a box of LEGO®. Removing a lid just an hour after a session can evoke a pungent, dirty stench that makes otherwise clean and shiny looking bricks smell really unpleasant, and makes playing with them a very unattractive proposition.

Each cleaning suggestion provided has been tested, but it is recommended that you carry out your preferred cleaning method on a small element first, and be aware that there is the possibility of damage being caused to both bricks and household appliances: *wash at your own risk!*

Hand wash

Add a mild detergent to warm water and soak the bricks in a bowl, bucket, sink or bath, depending on the size and quantity of the elements. Never use bleach.

Machine wash

Use a laundry mesh washing bag, or put bricks inside a pillow case, securing the end, and place in a washing machine. Set it to a delicate cycle, with no spin, to avoid damaging the bricks or the machine.

Rinse and dry

Rinse bricks under a tap, with a shower head or even a hosepipe! Shake dry using a sieve, salad spinner or colander. Leave to dry naturally at air temperature on a towel, draining board or hard surface, inside or outdoors. Never dry LEGO® in an oven, microwave or with a hairdryer.

Dusting

Dusting models can become tricky if not done regularly. Dusters may leave behind their own threads and residue, so the use of a soft brush to remove dust is recommended. Toothbrushes can be a bit too stiff, but a soft make-up or paint brush is ideal. A small handheld vacuum cleaner might prove effective; compressed air canisters are also helpful, but very expensive.

Refreshing

Use an antibacterial disinfectant spray, as it purports to kill off 99.9 per cent of bacteria, fragrances the boxes and the mist air-dries, making it very simple to use. Test the product first on a single element to check for possible damage.

LEGO® tips

Ole Kirk Christiansen's personal motto 'Det Bedste Er Ikke For Godt' translated as 'Only the Best is Good Enough' is at the heart of the LEGO® Company's design and production, as bricks connect with just the right amount of 'clutch power'.

Clutch power

This describes the ability of the bricks to click together snugly, whilst being easy to separate. The connection occurs when the studs on the top of a brick interlock with the tubes on the bottom of another.

How to describe a brick

LEGO® builders usually describe the size of a brick by its number of studs. For example, if a brick has two studs across and four going up (2×4), it's called a 2 by 4 brick.

Useful measurements

One LEGO® brick is equal in height to three LEGO® plates. In order to fit a LEGO® Minifigure into a model, the structure should be built at least five bricks high.

Brick separators

These come as standard in most of the large-sized boxes, and are *the* tool for separating bricks without needing to employ either teeth or fingernails! They are designed to push out pegs, remove tiles, and separate plates and bricks.

Helpful bricks for adding detail
SNOT bricks
An unpleasant sounding acronym, meaning LEGO® bricks with studs not on top. These are really useful for attaching a brick sideways (at 90 degrees to the usual orientation) and particularly helpful if a model requires a smooth, flat base with no studs.

Hinges
Excellent for creating movement and changing brick orientation.

Jumpers
Necessary for allowing an element to be centred in the middle of a brick.

Vertical plates
Mounting a plate in between two studs allows it to stand vertically at a right angle.

LEGO® glue (the interlocking brick technique)
This term refers to the way bricks should be placed in order to make the model more robust. It can be useful to let children look at the buildings or wall boundaries in their environment to see this in practice. Bricks should overlap from one row to another, so that a single brick cannot be removed without breaking apart whole sections of the wall.

How should the room be organised?

When working peripatetically it can be difficult to find an adequate space. What is of utmost importance, however, is that the designated location is constant each week, a dependable space in which to build, with privacy. In my experience, children do not wish to speak about their personal thoughts, feelings and worries if there is the possibility of being overheard or interrupted. The school library or music room is fine, but a table in the corridor or space in the corner of the hall is not conducive to a therapeutic environment.

The optimum set-up for a Thera-Build session is an area that is free from distractions, particularly from other people, who might wander by and cannot help but stop and show an interest in the process. Whilst it can be a positive experience for a child to have others taking notice, admiring models and expressing their wish to join in, it can also disrupt the creative activity, incite curious questioning, however well-intentioned, and disturb the process of relationship-building.

Ideally there would be access to fresh air, good lighting and a relatively comfortable area on the floor upon which to stretch out and build, a carpet or mat for instance. It is also necessary to have a hard surface on which to build, such as a wood floor, or access to a table, because it is more difficult to attach bricks to a baseplate on a spongy surface, such as carpet.

The space should be as simple and uncluttered as possible, so that the LEGO® takes precedence, and is more easily cleared away at the end. When working with more than one set, store the other(s) out of sight until they are required, so that the focus remains on the current activity.

If you are working with a group of children, then there should be sufficient space for everyone to build sizeable structures, and they should be situated in an area that allows for noisier, more energetic social play.

Thera-Build practitioners as facilitators

Practitioners must be playful, energetic and animated, with the ability to engage children in the Thera-Build process. It is essential to be consistent, congruent and able to attune to the needs of each child, helping and supporting their building of models and relationships, but not dominating, or forcing a build or activity. A passion, or at the very least a fondness for the plastic brick is essential!

- Be able to initiate interaction and entice a child into the activity.

- Be playful, fun-loving and relaxed.

- Be able to create a warm, secure and safe setting.

- Be curious, caring and genuinely interested in children.

- Be prepared to listen and appropriately respond to children's contributions.

- Be creative and adaptable.

- Be engaging, communicate clearly and involve children in positive social interaction.

- Be confident and firm when leading a session.

- Be fair, trustworthy, safe and predictable.

- Be open-minded and unprejudiced.

- Be aware of your own attachment style, your triggers and countertransference.

What to wear

Clothing should be comfortable and not restrictive, allowing the practitioner to adapt to the particular set of circumstances they find in placement. A simple uniform consisting of a 'Thera-Build' polo shirt, joggers and trainers allows for maximum freedom of movement and modesty, is practical if the floor is covered in mud, glue or glitter, and offers a consistency and familiarity that a child may instantly recognise upon arrival.

As the majority of interventions take place at school, and most children in the UK wear a school uniform, try to make children feel as comfortable as possible during a session by allowing them to remove their shoes, jumpers or blazers, and to loosen or remove their ties, so that they are not restricted in their play.

Be mindful of potential sensory triggers such as powerful scents.

Other adults

A Thera-Build session will either be a one-to-one between child and practitioner, or a small group of children with the practitioner, depending on the referral.

Every now and then it is necessary to have a support worker within a session if there are serious safety concerns, but this will change the dynamic of a Thera-Build session, so should only be exercised when there is a serious safeguarding risk.

Sometimes a piece of work is aimed around encouraging a parent to play and interact with their child(ren), so the adult relative would, of course, be present. It is vitally important that the adult feels safe to engage at their own level, and is not pressed into a forced exchange, judged or made to feel uncomfortable or inadequate in the session.

If a child were displaying particularly disturbing characteristics, other mental health agencies would observe the process to ensure that appropriate therapy is provided.

What to do if a child is resistant to the Thera-Build process

Initial refusal to engage in, or resistance to the process is unusual. If the Thera-Build practitioner is confident, energetic and supportive, and the LEGO® provided is suitably interesting and challenging, children usually engage in the building process willingly, or at most with a little gentle encouragement.

Resistance usually stems from a child's need to maintain a level of control. By giving the child control over their model-making, the LEGO® theme, the elements that they choose, and the freedom to adapt and modify their build as they see fit, most reluctance or refusal can be overcome effortlessly.

It is more common to find that as children begin to invest in the Thera-Build relationship, they will start to push their boundaries a few weeks in. This is a perfectly natural response and not one to be taken personally. Usually when a child begins to test the boundaries of the therapeutic relationship, trying out different vocabulary, moving unexpectedly around the room and so on, it is to assess the responses of the practitioner. The child needs to determine where the limits are set, that they are not prone to flux, change or whim and that the relationship is constant and dependable, in a bid to help them feel safe and secure.

Be consistent and calm, and where possible go with them and turn their behaviours into a playful experience. If you sense that a child is resisting a build because they are afraid of failure, then modify the task, or allow the child to adapt it to something that they find more comfortable and less intimidating.

Good session preparation that ensures a child is sufficiently stimulated and busy, engrossed in their building project and enjoying the process will reduce the likelihood of a child experimenting with challenging behaviours.

How to organise a Thera-Build session

Each Thera-Build session follows a flexible plan that encourages independence and decision-making. It is structured free-play that gives children the permission to make simple choices about their modelling and allows them to take a playful lead.

In many respects, a Thera-Build session acts as an extended anchoring exercise:

- Ask a child to rate their stress level.

- Spend time together building models and building connection.

- Review stress levels – expect positive change.

Introduction

An intervention using LEGO® would not be prescribed if a child had little or no interest in it as a medium, so we can safely assume that our first meeting will be positively received.

The Thera-Build practitioner should connect with the child in a playful, cheery manner, communicating that they are confident, responsible, safe and fun to be with. Always greet a child by name and with a smile. Beginning an interaction in this way, particularly when accompanied by eye contact and appropriate positive touch, conveys the message that 'you're special' and provides little opportunity for a child to dwell on any misgivings they might have about the process.

LEGO® check-in and check-out

It is good practice to 'check-in' with children at the beginning and end of each session. This might include using Minifigure emojis, colours, a single element choice, building a LEGO® emotional barometer or a quick 5-minute build (see Chapter 10).

The purpose of a check-in is to gain information on a child's state of mind at that moment. As children become more comfortable with this technique, they may talk at length about their feelings and experiences that day, how and maybe even why they believe their emotions shifted. This may provide rich conversation, become the main focus of the session or simply be a few minutes spent on developing a child's emotional intelligence.

LEGO® games

Often individual and small-group targets in a Thera-Build intervention involve the development of social skills, such as shared attention, taking turns, eye contact, patience, tolerance, compromise, speaking, listening and impulse control. As Thera-Build is inherently playful, LEGO® games are an excellent way to begin a session; by their very nature they encourage communication and nurture social and emotional development.

Children often relish designing and making their own LEGO® board games, which can become a construction and relationship-building project in its own right (see Chapter 10).

Main build

Due to the nature of Thera-Build, the LEGO® becomes the primary focus, which means that the pressure to make eye contact, speak or conform is immediately reduced. The child is unlikely to resist joining in or to verbalise reservations, because they have the freedom to build with a medium that they feel comfortable with and can have control over.

The practitioner provides the prompt into spontaneous playfulness, and a relationship actively begins to develop via the Thera-Build process of *build, play, listen, notice* and *respond*.

Wonder aloud

If a child seems reticent to talk, invite dialogue by saying 'You seem really happy', 'You look really sad', 'I noticed that…', 'I think you might feel…', or by 'wondering aloud' to increase their narrative, for example, 'I wonder what it would mean if…', 'I wonder what it would feel like when…', 'I wonder what x might say if…'

Encourage children to try to explain and name the sensations that they are experiencing, and provide opportunities for a child to tell and retell their experiences/stories, to help calm difficult emotions and to help a child begin to make sense of their narrative.

A positive approach

- Never force a child to engage with the process, merely encourage.

- Strike a balance between positively challenging a child to improve and develop construction skills, whilst keeping their building expectations realistic.

- Every model that a child produces has its own special qualities and uniqueness. Make sure to find them.

- Spend time observing and listening to each child talk freely about their MOC (my own creation) and take a genuine interest in the build and the commentary.

- Take care to ensure that children feel valued for who they are, not just for how well they build, interact or perform in session.

Close

Where possible, it is helpful to give a child ten minutes' notice before the session is due to finish, to prepare them for departure.

Try to make this a jolly thing: 'Oh no! Where has the time gone? It has been such fun building with you today, but it's nearly time for me to go.'

Packing up

When a child has invested their time and imagination into creating a model, feeling proud of what they have achieved, it can be upsetting to have to break it up. For children who have experienced repeated loss, this is especially difficult.

As a general rule, I ask the child(ren) to help pack away the unused LEGO®, but to leave their models complete, for photographing or display purposes. They might be protected and brought back the following week if a project is ongoing, or dismantled once the child has left. Never force a child to break their model into pieces, unless there is a positive therapeutic purpose for doing so.

Reconnection

Where possible, note something unique or significant to refer to in the following session, something specific to the individual; for example, 'You hurt your knee last week, how is it feeling now?' 'How did the dreaded spelling test you were worrying about go?'

This demonstrates that you remember your last session together, and have been holding the child in mind. It may be a simple recollection of the last Thera-Build session; for example, 'Here is your model from last week, I kept it safe as promised. My own children thought your build was awesome!'

Session logs

A record of each Thera-Build session should be made after each sitting. As play should be very natural and spontaneous, with the practitioner fully present during the session, note-taking or report writing should wait until the session has ended. The child should feel assured of the practitioner's presence and undivided attention, to help them to feel really connected.

After each session complete an entry into a child's log (see Appendix). This includes a helpful reminder of what building themes have already been covered, and the child's activity request for the next meeting. It leaves space for observations, quotes and concerns.

Session logs will form the basis of a Thera-Build assessment report, and should be completed with as much detail as is useful for the practitioner's records.

How to prepare a child for the end of a Thera-Build intervention

In an ideal world, we would know exactly how many sessions have been funded and the practitioner can organise and prepare for their exit in a healthy, supportive way. Unfortunately, this is not always the case in practice, and when circumstances change suddenly, it is not always something that can be prepared for.

Many children have experienced so many endings in their lives that have had such negative effects on their feelings of security, it almost seems cruel to offer a positive intervention, and build a trusting relationship, only to take it away because the funding has run out. In reality, with budgets so strained, being pragmatic and truthful with children about the intervention duration is the only credible approach.

The intervention may only last for a relatively short period of time, but during that period, the Thera-Build practitioner should have established a positive rapport with a child, mirrored them and helped the child to feel safe and cared about. This may be enough for a child to realise that there are adults available who are approachable and can be relied upon, to listen, understand, soothe and help them.

When brought in by a school or parent to work with an individual child as an intermediary, Thera-Build can be an incredibly powerful process in helping both sides understand each other. Thera-Build practitioners may prove to be a temporary but vital link in order to bring about positive change.

In a setting where Thera-Build is delivered by the pastoral team, there is much more scope for weaning a child from the process. As a practitioner continues to monitor and support a child's progress, and ensures that they are coping more positively, weekly sessions may become fortnightly, then monthly, according to individual need.

Be aware that the last session with a child may be an anti-climactic experience. It can seem that a child is backing off, snubbing or punishing a practitioner for leaving them. Alternatively, it might be an emotional, poignant and tearful session, when a child openly appears to be feeling the loss, will ask lots of questions and often orchestrate a spontaneous cuddle.

Self-care for practitioners

When spending a significant amount of time with children who may be highly charged, impulsive and volatile, practitioners must manage their own stress levels, anxiety and exhaustion, to avoid burn-out or compassion fatigue. Support at home is hugely beneficial; but seeking regular supervision is a basic professional requirement for Thera-Build practitioners.

Chapter 10

LEGO® Activities

Check-in and check-out activities

Emojis

Download a set of emoji cards from www.build-happy.co.uk and laminate them. Lay them out on a flat surface, and let a child choose the one that most reflects how they are feeling.

Enlarge emojis and place them on the wall, with some associated emotions vocabulary. Provide a playful spinner for children to rotate, to indicate how they are feeling.

If the setting is appropriate, a child's face or Minifigure avatar could be laminated and temporarily fastened to the emoji that best describes their current feelings.

Colours

Which colour brick matches how you are feeling today?

Select a brick

Choose a brick that fits with how you are feeling right now.

5-minute build

Take 5 minutes to build a quick model to show how you are feeling at the moment.

Brick towers

1. Give children three bricks and ask them to arrange their bricks on a small plate at the beginning of a session. The brick on the top acts as the indicator signal. Green means I am okay, yellow means I am struggling and red means I need help.

2. Provide children with ten bricks and a small baseplate. Allow children to build a tower to represent their state of arousal. A visual, brick-built 1–10 check-in exercise.

Thera-Build traffic lights

Build a traffic light model that remains static, in any way a child likes. Each child can choose how they use the model to best depict their state of mind, for example, a brick, Minifigure or photo marker.

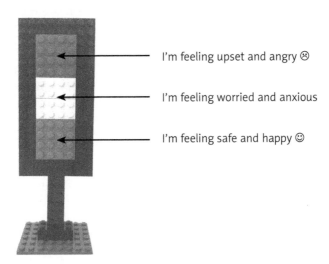

I'm feeling upset and angry ☹

I'm feeling worried and anxious

I'm feeling safe and happy ☺

Build a LEGO® emotional barometer

This is a helpful visual aid that displays an awareness of changing moods and emotions. You can ask the child(ren):

- If they know what a barometer is. (An instrument that measures air pressure, and is used to forecast changes in the weather.) It may be helpful to show some examples of real barometers and to have a collection of feelings cards available.

- To think about how a barometer could be used, to show the level of intensity of feelings that a child might be experiencing.

- To design and build their own emotional barometer from LEGO®, in any way that they like. Children should make colour choices for the different sections, to indicate increasing levels of arousal, to improve self-awareness and enrich their own feelings vocabulary.

- To discuss how it feels to be at a particular level, and the likely behaviours that might occur.

- To think of beneficial ways to change state.

Furious and enraged

Angry and aggressive

Panicky and scared

Anxious and frustrated

Tense and uncomfortable

Sad or confused

Calm and content

Relaxed and happy

Thera-Build encourages the use of imagination, creativity and purposeful conversation, in a playful building context. It is another way to work with children to help build relationships, and generate understanding.

LEGO® is central to the therapeutic process, and is not to be used just as a 'reward' at the end of a session.

Energisers

One way to begin a Thera-Build session is to provide a quick building activity, or simple LEGO® problem-solving exercise.

Chopsticks

Transfer a small pile of LEGO® elements from one bowl to another, using a pair of chopsticks.

Seamless symmetry

Take a baseplate each, and build a vertical line of bricks down the centre. Both child and practitioner separately build a LEGO® pattern on one side of a board, and then swap plates with each other. Build on to make the other side symmetrical.

Drop zone

Assemble ten LEGO® bricks of your choice, so that when they are dropped from a tabletop, they will not break apart. You have 3 minutes – go!

Build a shape

Decide on a 2D or 3D shape that you each try to build with LEGO®, for example, cube, triangle, sphere.

Minifigure construction

Build your own Minifigure from a selection of heads, legs, torsos and accessories.

Truck topple

Take two pairs of wheels and join them with a plate to make a simple vehicle chassis. Take it in turns to add one 2×4 brick to the plate, in any direction, then roll it to the other player. Whoever causes the truck to topple over, loses.

LEGO® jar

Fill a jar with lots of LEGO® elements. Ask the child to guess how many pieces are inside. They can touch and turn the jar to help with their observations, but the lid must remain on.

Random creator

Scoop up a random selection of LEGO® elements in a plastic cup or bowl. Create a model from the brick assortment.

Animal 'feely' bag

Put a collection of LEGO® or DUPLO® animals into a bag, pillowcase or box, and ask the child to feel one, touch and describe it, and see if they can identify what animal is hiding inside.

IdentiKit

Create two identical collections of bricks, one for the child and one for the practitioner. Work back to back, set a short time frame, no more than 5 minutes, and build a model. Afterwards compare and contrast your builds, identifying and celebrating their differences.

Energiser activity cards

Build a fish	Build a vehicle	Build a robot	Build a castle
Build an animal	Build a house	Build a boat	Build a sport
Build a pyramid	Build a spaceship	Build something you can eat	Build a flower/plant
Build your first initial	Build a model in just 1 minute!	Build a model beginning with 'M'	Build with your eyes shut for 3 minutes
Build a model using only one brick colour	Build a model with only one hand!	Build an underwater scene	Build a model beginning with 'R'
Build a candle	Build a household object	Build your favourite story	Build a character
Build a wish	Build the seaside	Build a cave	Build an insect

Sensory experiences

Some children find it calming simply to touch the LEGO® elements, without specifically building anything. Let them feel it, click it, sort it, connect it, demolish it.

Finger gliding

Set up a suitably sized box of LEGO® so that a child can glide their fingers over the top of it. Smaller 1×1 and 1×2 pieces are the most effective size to use, as they have more fluidity and don't hurt!

Delving

Provide a large box of elements for a child to root through, for no particular purpose. They may well find a focus for their delving, and this may become changeable – simply support the process.

Burrowing

For some children, burrowing their hands right down into the bottom of a container, swirling their hands around under the LEGO® and squeezing the bricks can act as a tension reliever.

Scoop pots

Provide a variety of containers that children can use to collect, shake and pour the LEGO®. For example, a yoghurt pot, plastic cup, flowerpot with a hole in the bottom, small bottle or large lid.

Dropping

Clutching handfuls of LEGO® and releasing them, so that they drop back into the container, can feel really soothing. The rhythmic movement and process of watching the bricks tumble, and control over the dropping speed, can really help to calm a child. Beware of dropping from a height, however, because hard plastic hurts and scattered bricks make packing away more difficult.

Find me

Searching for one specific element can be a very mindful activity, as children rummage through a LEGO® collection with one particular focus. Look out for signs of frustration, however, as this can tip over into an exasperating experience for some.

Sorting

Having control and order over a brick assortment may bring comfort to some children. Let them choose how they wish to sort the bricks, for example, by colour, shape, size, texture, theme. Provide separate containers or plastic trays with dividers to help isolate collections.

Sensory construction site

Spread LEGO® across a large tray and provide, or build, LEGO® construction vehicles, for example, diggers and dumper trucks. Use them to dig trenches and transport bricks. Try other sensory materials in the tray, such as sand, small beads or gravel.

Minifigure lucky dip

Add a quantity of Minifigure heads, legs and torsos to a box. Fill the box with a contrasting material, such as shredded paper or foam peanuts, and ask the child to feel around in the box and collect Minifigure parts to assemble. How many complete LEGO® people can they make?

Gel bags

Add some clear soap or hair gel to a ziplock bag, and pop in some 1×1 LEGO® studs of different colours. Squeeze out the air and seal the bag. Using their fingers on the outside of the bag, ask a child to group the pieces inside, in any way that they like.

Feeling calm

Some children have little or no experience of what it actually feels like to be calm, particularly those children who come from chaotic households, who regularly arrive at school in a state of distress, and are unsure what they will be returning to at the end of the day.

Allowing a child sufficient time and space to know what it feels like to stop, take a breath and feel the sensations of calm and relaxation flood their bodies and minds may be life-changing for a child who is constantly in 'fight or flight' mode. Sometimes a child is so exhausted that laying them down in a safe space and covering them in a warm blanket is the most fitting response. Let the child rest quietly, play some soothing background music or read them a story to evoke feelings of calm, which must be physically felt to be truly understood.

Spend five minutes at the beginning of the school day, just before play time, after lunch or before home time to practise calming skills for all children, when they are not in an obvious state of anger or anxiety, so that it becomes part of the normal routine and classroom culture.

Thera-Build calm box

Building a Thera-Build calm box together with a child has many therapeutic benefits. As the practitioner physically constructs the box and its contents along with the child, there are lots of opportunities for connection, mirroring, merger, twinship and initiating. When finished, the calm box is a unique and personal resource for a child to use to support self-regulation when required.

Take an old shoebox, wrap, line and decorate it together, letting the child choose the materials, colours and embellishments, to make it unique and special to them.

Include objects and activities to engage the child in visual/hands-on pursuits, to relieve tension, and encourage deep breathing.

LEGO®-themed calm box suggested contents

1. A box of LEGO® for sorting or building.

2. Make a handheld windmill, or kaleidoscope, decorated and personalised by the child.

3. Include a bottle of bubbles, party blower, straw for blowing paint, whistle or harmonica.

4. A LEGO® book, magazine or encyclopaedia that can be flicked through or read quietly.

5. A collection of LEGO® images for colouring and some pencils or crayons.

6. LEGO® jigsaws. Let the child choose the picture, and make your own for them to complete.

7. A LEGO® calm down jar. Shake it up and watch all the pieces gradually settle.

8. A stress ball made from cornflour and a balloon, with a Minifigure face drawn on to it.

9. LEGO® cards, quizzes, fact sheets, stickers or puzzle books.

10. A LEGO® rain-shaker, fidget spinner or 'Find-It' game.

Back into balance

When a child has had experience of being in a positive and desirable emotional state, we need to prepare and assist them to access this state for themselves. They may well require a lot of coaching and support initially, to recognise what is happening inside their bodies as they begin to dysregulate. They will also need to trust that the Thera-Build practitioner is there to help comfort and protect them, as their right brain starts to take charge.

It may be that a child deploys their calm box in an effort to self-regulate, or they may be able to divert their brain to their safe space independently, or with gentle encouragement. When the child's arousal levels have reduced, the practitioner can start to carefully divert the child from right- to left-brain activity, by playfully asking them to spell their name backwards, or to recite the ten times table for instance, before moving on.

Building resilience

A person's resilience describes their capacity to recover quickly from any obstacle or difficulty that they are faced with – their 'bounce-back-ability' from a situation.

LEGO® construction can be a great metaphor for life's changes, as models are built, taken apart and reconstructed over time.

The LEGO® building process itself may also build resilience, as young people strive to create a model, and face frustrations or complications during the activity; for example, frustration at not being able to find a specific element, disappointment if a part won't connect properly or exasperation when a section collapses, or breaks. This reflects the normal patterns of human life, as we ride the ups and downs of everyday physical and emotional experiences.

Thera-Build does not seek or require building perfection. Therefore, if a model falls to pieces, a child accidentally knocks it over or poor construction causes it to collapse, children should understand that this happens regularly to us all, and is a completely normal part of the building process. Managing the irritation through co- or self-regulation, via a slow, deep breath, a few choice words, holding their head in their hands for a few seconds and perhaps even a little humour, children can be taught to see it as a new and positive opportunity that has arisen. It may be the chance to alter the original model, to create another that is more strong and robust, even if it means abandoning a build altogether and starting afresh.

The main point is that a child should not regard themselves as hopeless, or as a failure, who can't and won't ever be able to do something successfully. Through playful activity, in a safe climate, with no pressure to achieve an ideal, and the practitioner building beside them, modelling those same mishaps and frustrations, children can learn that we all make mistakes, face disappointment and experience impatience, but it is the way we respond that can make a very real difference to the outcome.

By building trust and assembling a bank of positive strategies to help young people to seek help and to talk about what is happening, they will begin to develop resilience.

Measures of psychological well-being

To measure the impact of a Thera-Build intervention, consider using the Rosenberg Self-Esteem Scale (Rosenberg 1989), which is still widely used as a reliable and valid tool for assessing levels of self-esteem.

Complete the same assessment at both the first and last Thera-Build sessions to get a numeric/quantitive indicator of change.

This is not a test with right or wrong answers, but a questionnaire designed to measure self-worth.

Ask the child to complete it as honestly and truthfully as they can, to help you, as practitioner, to get to know them a little better.

The practitioner may read the statements aloud for a child if required.

Calculating scores

Scoring for statements 1, 3, 4, 7, 10		Scoring for statements 2, 5, 6, 8, 9	
Points	Response	Points	Response
3	Strongly agree	0	Strongly agree
2	Agree	1	Agree
1	Disagree	2	Disagree
0	Strongly disagree	3	Strongly disagree

Understanding scores

- There are ten sentences on a four-point scale.

- The scale ranges from 0 to 30.

- Higher scores indicate higher self-esteem.

- Scores between 15 and 25 are considered to be within the normal range.

- Scores below 15 suggest low self-esteem.

Rosenberg Self-Esteem Scale

Here is a list of statements dealing with your feelings about yourself.

Read each sentence, and circle the head that best shows how strongly you agree, or disagree with each statement.

1. On the whole I am satisfied with myself			
Strongly agree	Agree	Disagree	Strongly disagree

2. At times I think I am no good at all			
Strongly agree	Agree	Disagree	Strongly disagree

3. I feel that I have a number of good qualities			
Strongly agree	Agree	Disagree	Strongly disagree

4. I am able to do things as well as most other people.			
Strongly agree	Agree	Disagree	Strongly disagree

5. I feel I do not have much to be proud of			
Strongly agree	Agree	Disagree	Strongly disagree

6. I feel useless at times			
Strongly agree	Agree	Disagree	Strongly disagree

7. I think that I am alright, and as good as everyone else			
Strongly agree	Agree	Disagree	Strongly disagree

8. I wish I could have more respect for myself			
Strongly agree	Agree	Disagree	Strongly disagree

9. I often think I am a failure			
Strongly agree	Agree	Disagree	Strongly disagree

10. Most of the time I feel good about myself			
Strongly agree	Agree	Disagree	Strongly disagree

The stressor/worry jar

A simple way to identify and measure specific stressors or worries is to provide children with a variety of different sized LEGO® bricks and a jar. The child can identify individual stressors/worries and select a brick to represent its size: big worries onto big bricks and smaller stressors onto smaller bricks. Provide prompts if a child is struggling. For example, think about a worry you have at home, school, about somebody else, etc.

- As they are placed into the jar, talk briefly about each one. This can provide valuable intel on which worries need to be prioritised.

- Choose one brick to further explore. What is the issue? What might help to soothe this feeling? Is there anything a young person could do differently to change the situation?

- Explore different strategies for reducing the magnitude of feeling each brick contains, and investigate whether some bricks could be removed altogether.

- Avoid overwhelming a child, by working on just one targeted aspect at a time.

- If it is helpful, record what each brick represents by colouring and labelling the brick templates, which are included in the downloadable resources.

One brick on top of another

Sometimes a young person may feel so overwhelmed by the number of things piling up on top of them that they speak in generalisations: 'It's all too much', 'Everything is a mess', 'Nobody understands what I am going through', 'I can't do anything right', or 'Everybody hates me'.

One way to organise their thoughts and help to identify the various issues is to start by placing one brick on a baseplate to represent one thought, stressor, area of concern, feeling, consequence, challenge, fear, emotion or action, and to name it. Repeat the process by taking a further brick and placing it on top of the other, until a tower is formed.

The height of the tower will indicate the number of preoccupations the young person is currently juggling. It can be helpful for the practitioner to jot these down as a child is building, for reference, without interrupting the flow of the child's thoughts or dialogue.

The resilience see-saw

The ability of a child to regulate their behaviour hinges upon their ability to manage stress. When helping children to understand a little about stress, we might build LEGO® see-saws together, so that we can physically build and observe those things that add stress, and those that can reduce it.

Ask the child to write their stressors onto stickers and fix them to the LEGO® bricks. Be aware that there may be hidden stressors involved that a child considers normal, if their baseline is already high. Sometimes a brick that one might assume would be a relaxer is actually regarded by the child as a stressor. Explore them.

When the stress load begins to increase, we need to teach children positive strategies for bringing about balance.

1. Discuss ways of decreasing the size of the stressor.

2. Can we eliminate some of the stressor bricks altogether?

3. Could we move some of the stressors into relaxers?

Thera-Build emotional first aid kit

Set a child the task of recording their stressors and how they currently handle them; acknowledging any coping tactics that a child can identify, even the harmful ones. Discuss and gently guide towards those strategies that are safe and protective, for inclusion in their own Thera-Build first aid kit. A template for this activity is provided in the downloadable resources.

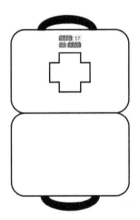

A sensory scavenger hunt

A mindful way to encourage attention, building, movement and conversation, to alleviate anxiety.

THERA ☺ BUILD			
LEGO® Scavenger Hunt Build something...			
To balance on your head	Smooth	That rattles	Using just one colour
That uses two shades of the same colour	A Minifigure can sit in	Bigger than your shoe	With four legs
Round	Wider than your hand-span	Spiky	A Minifigure can hide underneath
Longer than your thumb	Beginning with the letters L-E-G-O	That fits in the palm of your hand	To throw a beanbag into
That contains all the colours of the rainbow	Transparent	With equal sized sides	That can balance on your nose

Self-esteem memos

As a child's core beliefs significantly affect their levels of confidence, write and record positive messages for a child to keep. They may come from the child themselves, the practitioner, another child, a member of staff or a family member, but should be authentic and sincere.

Mount them in their building booklet, pop them into a child's calm box, use a plastic tub or construct a LEGO® safe to store them inside.

Encourage the child to write three positive beliefs about themselves onto a brick and laminate it so that it can be carried around with them in their pocket, bag or pencil case.

I believe that I am good at:
....
....
....

I believe that I am a(n) .... person, because ....
....
....

This message is from ....
to say ....
....
....

Model responses

It might be helpful to build a scenario with a child, depicting a particular event that you can explore together. This could be a purely fictitious incident, or a conflict situation that has directly involved the child. You may ask a child to think back to a time when they felt a particular emotion, and to use the LEGO® bricks to build that emotion, for example, when a child felt lonely, excited, frightened, surprised, hopeless, motivated, unhappy, valuable, scared, happy, shocked, angry, mischievous or powerful.

Remember that models do not have to be exact representations; the bricks may act as metaphors, with one brick symbolising a person, idea, emotion, feeling or place. The size, colour or shape of the element may provide clues about what it depicts, but listen to what the child is telling you, as their model is whatever they say it is.

Build the scene, including as much or as little detail as necessary, and use LEGO® Minifigures to role-play what happened. Support children to express any feelings that they may have difficulty verbally articulating. It might be that a child is able to speak more comfortably through a third person (Minifigure) than directly to the practitioner, particularly in the early days of the therapeutic relationship. Explore with a child how they felt, how they acted and how others responded.

LEGO® is an excellent playful tool for providing a narrative, and the process provides ample opportunities to glimpse a child's inner world.

Create stop motion animations

An exciting way to develop LEGO® model scenarios is to animate situations, using an online stop motion movie app. These are fun to make, provide a record of what the child has done, and can be enjoyed by other children for entertainment and educational purposes.

Minifigure thought and speech bubbles

Minifigures can be of tremendous value in role-play situations. They may be used to help a child reflect their own thoughts and emotions, to add dialogue, to view a situation from the perspective of another, to build and discuss scenarios, to talk about what might have happened before or after an event, to model alternative responses or to challenge negative statements about self.

By giving the thoughts and words to a Minifigure, it can help to create a safe distance from which a child might explore.

- Photocopy the thought and speech bubbles onto stiff paper or card.

- Cut them out and write on them.

- Attach them to a Minifigure by removing its head and slotting it onto the torso.

- Secure in position by replacing the head.

- Build a scene, and create a thought process or dialogue with the Minifigures.

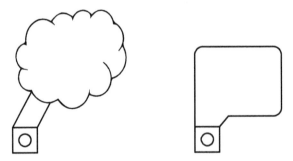

Games

Thera-Build uses LEGO® to play, entertain, challenge, soothe or distract children. Use games as a simple way to initiate conversation, learn about sharing, to practise rhythmic turn-taking and to improve visual memory.

The LEGO® Group released a range of brick-built board games in 2009, a theme that ran for nearly four years, but is now a retired product. An interchangeable die element was included in every set, and the games were designed to be modified by the players to extend game-play. Check for second-hand availability.

Alternatively design and build games from LEGO® for, or together with a child, to trial new skills or goals, using a theme or activity that interests or motivates them.

Ideas for making LEGO® games

Instead of building a game completely out of LEGO® bricks, which can be very time-consuming, try the following.

Brick the pieces

Take a standard board game, such as snakes and ladders, but use LEGO® bricks or Minifigures as the playing tokens. A LEGO® die could replace the original. Try to re-create a classic board game with LEGO®, for example, Tic-Tac-Toe (noughts and crosses) or Ludo. Play 'Kim's Game' where different LEGO® elements or a variety of Minifigures are placed on a baseplate, memorised, then covered up, as one is removed. The players have to identify the missing piece(s).

Downloadable track templates

Search online for free board game downloadable templates. Select a track, make up some simple instructions, decorate it with a LEGO® theme, laminate and play together.

Board game makeover

Take an unused or cheap second-hand board game and give it a LEGO® makeover. Select a LEGO® theme, adapt the location spaces using paint or other materials, make new player tokens and invent a complete set of rules.

LEGO® cards

Make a set of cards to play different games with, such as snap, memory pairs or happy families.

More lively activities

To create movement, cooperation and even competition, try out these ideas.

Pot shot

Throw LEGO® elements into the correctly coloured pots, or throw hoops over LEGO® towers.

Marble mazes/marble runs

These are exciting to construct, and keep a child entertained and focused whilst building. They are fun to play with too!

Treasure hunts

This can be a simple hiding game, or a more complex adventure involving clues.

LEGO® graffiti

Screw large baseplates to a wall, and let children free-build all over them with bricks of their choice.

Board games planner

Create-Build-Play! Board games made of LEGO®

Discuss it:
- What type of game would you like to build?
- Which theme will you choose?
- What is the aim of the game? How do players win?
- How many players is it for?
- How much of the game will be based on luck? Skill?

Design it:
- Sketch a rough board design.
- Add a start and finish.
- Where do players move/land?
- What must players do?
- Write out the basic rules.

Build it:
- Build the board.
- Add elements for interesting game-play.
- Create your player pieces.
- Construct your dice or spinner.
- Include any extra details.

Test/tweak it:
- Did it play well?
- Was it too easy/too hard?
- Were there other ways to win?
- Could the rules be broken?
- How long did it take to play?
- Do you need to make any changes?
- Do you need to build anything else?

Play it:
- Name your game.
- Play it together.
- Try out other games.
- Enjoy! ☺

Ten LEGO® building ideas

Through the imaginations of both child and practitioner, the building possibilities are truly endless.

1. Animals: jungle, domestic, wild, farmyard, zoo, arctic, fish, insects.

2. Buildings: houses, castles, dungeons, towers, pyramids, igloos, stadiums.

3. Recreation: playgrounds, fair rides, sports pitches, landscapes, shops.

4. Transportation: cars, boats, buses, hovercrafts, monster trucks, transporters.

5. Things that fly: birds, hot air balloons, spaceships, helicopters, aeroplanes, rockets.

6. Minifigures: take them outside and position them in a real-world setting.

7. Food: cakes, breakfast, fruit, lunchboxes, cookies, snacks, sweets, dinner.

8. Objects: furniture, household appliances, gadgets, flags, pencil holders, door plaques.

9. Structures: bridges, catapults, road networks, windmills, aqueducts, piers, pylons.

10. Seasonal: builds related to seasons and holidays, for example Halloween, Christmas, summer.

Ten LEGO® play themes

1. Space

2. Desert Adventure

3. Pirates

4. Robots

5. Fairy Kingdom

6. Under the sea

7. 1-2-3-emergency!

8. Down on the farm

9. The Arctic Circle

10. Super Hero city.

Ten LEGO® art ideas

1. Build LEGO® mosaics from 1×1 bricks.

2. Construct/decorate a frame from bricks that can be used to border a photograph.

3. Build a LEGO® stationery pot to store pens and pencils.

4. Make jewellery, such as necklaces or rings, by gluing, or threading bricks.

5. Build Christmas decorations, for example, LEGO® candy-canes, or brick baubles to hang on the tree.

6. Design and make your own LEGO® badge, cap or T-shirt.

7. Melt down wax and add to a mould to make your own LEGO® crayons.

8. Make LEGO® felt boards for play or display.

9. Create a LEGO® colouring wall using either a large wall mural or smaller pictures to mount.

10. Make paper doll chains using a Minifigure-shaped template or cut out LEGO® snowflakes.

Ten LEGO® baking/food ideas

1. Bake a simple biscuit recipe and ice it with a LEGO® theme.

2. Make a Minifigure head lollipop by pushing a marshmallow onto a stick and decorating it.

3. Prepare jelly bricks from a mould, or layer up different coloured jellies in individual pots.

4. Bake cupcakes with food dye, or decorate them with a fondant LEGO® brick.

5. Craft chocolate bricks or ice-lollies from a LEGO® mould.

6. Create rectangle pizza slices with pepperoni arranged on top to look like LEGO® studs.

7. Cut a slice of cheese into the shape of a Minifigure head and mount upon a cracker.

8. Assemble colourful fruit skewers in primary colour arrangements.

9. Compile colourful raw vegetable skewers.

10. Cook mini brick-shaped loaves of bread.

Creative techniques

When children start to develop emotional intelligence, the evidence suggests that they become less volatile, less anxious and withdrawn, their sleep quality improves, they get along better with peers and staff at school, and their academic performance improves.

During a Thera-Build intervention, a whole array of creative techniques may be used to develop emotional intelligence. They are generally used when there is no obvious solution to a problem and when a young person is overwhelmed by emotion or confusion. These techniques, using LEGO® playfully, may prove helpful in bringing unconscious processes into the spotlight.

Often behaviour defends the part of a child that is hurting. That wounded part is hiding somewhere underneath, in need of healthy resolution. The practitioner must listen to, and try to understand that damaged part in order to raise a child's self-awareness, and to support that young person, as they begin to heal from their earlier experiences.

Obviously, any disclosures that carry a safeguarding risk must be reported to the relevant body immediately. Any revelations such as physical or sexual abuse, self-harm or suicidal thoughts, and other specific mental health issues, such as hallucinations, compulsive, repetitive behaviours or intense mood swings, must be referred on to a qualified therapist.

Let us consider some creative techniques that could be undertaken in a Thera-Build intervention:

Build your name with LEGO®

Provide a selection of baseplates and bricks, and let each child choose the elements they want, to build their name, in any way that they like. For example, flat, in plate form, standing up in 3D, just initials, a nickname or even pictorially.

It is fascinating to observe the colour choice, brick placement, size and creativity involved in this activity, and to think about what that might mean for each young person.

It is certainly a good opportunity for a child to open up about their name, and what it means to them. For example, do they have a different family name to those that they live with? Is the child's name unusual and often mispronounced? Do they prefer an abbreviated version of their name?

Building the family dynamic with LEGO®

Give each child access to a baseplate and a range of LEGO® elements, but not in huge volume. Ask the child to select a brick, or to click a few together to represent themselves. Suggest that they place the model of themselves in the centre of the baseplate.

Next, ask the child to think of the people who are closest to them. Ask them to represent each person in brick form, and to attach them to the plate, in relation to themselves, and in a position that feels right or comfortable.

Thera-Build does not advocate using these models to interpret the actions or motivations of others, offer explanations or make any judgements. This technique is designed as an activity to 'provoke feeling' about a person or situation, to promote dialogue and to provide a window into a child's family dynamic.

By projecting their inner world into a model, using different elements to represent the important people in their life, and moving them around in a 3D space, it can offer some clarity or perspective on past events, or a current situation. A LEGO® remote control could be used to modify the scene, by pausing a story, replaying a part, giving a Minifigure the opportunity for a monologue, removing or replacing a character, changing the script, etc.

If appropriate, you could use the model to build more detailed scenarios as they are remembered, and to rewrite them, perhaps adding a new voice to a character, changing dialogue or altering behaviours. However, this should only be undertaken when your alliance is strong and secure, as these representations can evoke powerful emotions.

There is some emotional distance created in this activity, providing some protection for a child, as they can talk about and manipulate characters that are physically removed from themselves, making it safer to explore. If the practitioner considers it a suitable extension, they might provide an alternative memory in which a child's needs are met, in order to aid recovery.

Build a super hero shield

Frequently children will express frustration and anger when they arrive at a Thera-Build session by blaming another child or member of staff for the onset of their rage. In discussion, it often transpires that they feel under attack, verbally or physically, by another person, and so lash out in response.

It might be helpful to introduce the idea of a super hero shield that they could use to protect themselves and defend against the behaviours in others that they find the most irritating or distressing.

First, build a shield out of LEGO®. This may be any size, shape and style that the child chooses. As it is a 'super hero' shield, it may well have a variety of fantasy gadgets or special functions.

Next, role-play a situation that has occurred, either as child and practitioner, or with Minifigures.

Role-play the scenario again, but this time, allow the child to use the shield to protect themselves. For example, to deflect a kick or punch by placing the shield in a physically defensive position, or by holding the shield out in front of them to rebound a shout or nasty comment, providing breathing space, whilst the child thinks of a more appropriate response, rather than reacting instinctively and aggressively.

Once this proves successful, move on to the concept that the super hero shield can be with a child at all times, in their mind. Provide opportunities for the child to practise deflecting comments and other provocations, rather than absorbing them and feeling the associated hurt and anger.

Build a safe space

Spend some time discussing and thinking about what feeling 'safe' actually feels like; be aware that sadly, some children might have limited experience of this state of mind.

Ask the children to think about somewhere they have previously felt safe, a place where they might go to if they need some comfort or reassurance, or even an imaginary safe place. What would it look like? Feel like? Who would be there?

As children contemplate and visualise, allow them to lie comfortably on the floor or a beanbag, and encourage them to close their eyes, so that they can focus their attention on their safe space.

When appropriate, gently pose some sensory questions about the safe place:

- What can you see?

- What can you hear?

- What can you touch? How does it feel?

- Are there any unusual smells?

- Are there any special tastes?

- How do you feel in your safe space?

If the child seems relaxed and calm, allow them to spend a few more minutes experiencing these peaceful sensations before asking them to open their eyes. As they re-enter full consciousness, ask the child to tell you about some of the feelings they experienced whilst in their safe place.

Invite the child to construct their safe space from LEGO®. This could be a symbolic interpretation or a detailed build, depending on the child. Use the model as a visual aid for further discussion.

Practitioners should ensure that they are listening to, and actively trying to understand the young person as they build, to strengthen the therapeutic relationship. The act of playing and building together should ignite a powerful and enjoyable sense of connection and delight in one another's company, as each person physically attunes to the other.

Thera-Build scenarios

Use these ideas to build realistic but ambiguous scenes as an explorative activity to prompt conversation and observe the thoughts, emotional responses and attitudes of the child. Pay attention to any potential triggers or themes with which a child may be preoccupied.

Each scenario contains a variety of Minifigures, settings and situations. These are merely suggestions, and practitioners should feel free to build individual scenarios as befits their individual circumstances. It is also advisable to introduce the idea by building some simple, non-contentious scenes first, to make the process safe and playful. Prompt children to build their own scenarios for you to discuss also.

Encourage the child to discuss what they can see and to tell a story about each model. Consider:

- What do you think is happening in the model right now?

- Who do you think each character might be?

- What is each character thinking/feeling/saying/doing?

- What happened before this scene do you suppose?

- What do you think is going to happen afterwards?

Let children build their responses with LEGO® to help them organise the narrative. Use multiple boards if necessary.

A car driving away with a Minifigure behind the wheel and a child on the back seat	A male and female Minifigure facing each other with hands raised	An open door into a brick room, where different elements have been scattered
A Minifigure lying face down on the floor	The back of a Minifigure holding suitcases	A Minifigure, standing alone amongst a rocky landscape
A sad/tearful Minifigure face looking out of a window	A group of Minifigures sitting around a table	A Minifigure child climbing a staircase
A kitchen scene with food being prepared, one Minifigure standing and another sitting	A Minifigure on the phone, either checking messages or talking	A child Minifigure hiding under a table or behind a sofa

Chapter 11

Final Thoughts

The reason that I find Thera-Build so exciting (apart from the fact that I get to play regularly with LEGO®) is that I spend time with children, who are all so precious and unique. It is a privilege and a joy to spend time playing and building together with them, and it is never dull!

My main piece of advice is to be flexible. Of course, you must enter a session with a plan and your themed bricks, but don't be fearful or despondent if the session goes off on a different tangent. That is the exciting part! It is obvious that what works for one child will not work for another; similarly, something can work out really well, but not in the way you had originally intended. Of course, the opposite is also true, so be alert during a session, and don't be afraid to experiment and change direction as and when necessary. There is no rule book for this, just experience and practice.

> **Case Example**: Scott, aged 2, was amongst a group of toddlers I was working with. I tipped out a huge box of DUPLO® on the floor and began to encourage them all to build, but Scott showed no interest in the bricks, except to walk amongst the DUPLO® and kick it. He went on to hit the models out of the hands of the other children. Scott made no sounds, and his face displayed no animation.
>
> After a few minutes of modelling behaviour with the rest of the group, I turned around and discovered that Scott had climbed into my storage box. He had wriggled right down to the bottom and was trying to put the lid on; but he did not succeed because he was taller than the box. For about ten minutes I played with him in the box, putting the lid

over his head and peering through it (as it was transparent), making him smile. I then sang 'Row Your Boat' with him, as I rocked the box back and forth and went on to 'fly' him out of the box.

The DUPLO® was not important at all; it was the relationship, the connection, which was vital for Scott. When he felt safe, he began to giggle and repeatedly requested 'again', until my arms were too exhausted to lift him any more. I suggested that we play with the DUPLO® instead, and Scott was then able to rejoin the rest of the children, without destroying their builds, and began to put bricks together himself. As social creatures, the human brain is wired to connect safely, and that was what Scott needed to feel before he could join in appropriately with the rest of the group.

Bear in mind that children who have been abused or neglected have every reason to be wary of adults. Where shame is embedded, there will also be an underlying fear that, once they connect to a practitioner and open up to the Thera-Build experience, the adult will discover what the child is really like, and abandon them.

When children have been traumatised, they can be afraid to feel any emotions, as they can be too hurtful and/or lead to a further loss of control. Children may therefore try to forget about, or hide how scared or angry they feel, for fear of the consequences when they are triggered. A Thera-Build practitioner must not push this process, or force a child to engage.

In my experience when a child does begin to connect and perhaps discloses something that pains them, or makes them feel vulnerable, their anxiety may well be high the next time we meet. They might be wondering if they have to pick up where they left off, have reservations about a further heavy or intense session, worry that they said too much last time and what the consequences of that disclosure might mean, or feel guilty if they have spoken out against a significant adult in the home or at school.

Mirroring a child in the succeeding session, getting back in tune with them and allowing them to go at their own pace, providing little prompts where appropriate, to let them know that you are present and available to respond to their needs, keeps the next session light, and gives a child permission to feel safe and in control of what, how and when they continue to share.

To try to improve a young person's emotional intelligence and reduce their feelings of stress, anxiety or depression, we need to embark on a journey of exploration together, but this is only possible when the child feels safe and secure enough to participate.

Final checklist

- Be relaxed and meet the child at their physical level to appear approachable and accessible.

- Smiling is a very simple way to express your joy in the Thera-Build process, and can be infectious. Children will study facial expressions to learn more about a practitioner.

- Use appropriate eye contact and positive touch with caution.

- Non-verbal messages are as significant as those that are verbalised, and should be congruent. Body language should be open, and correspond with your words.

- Look out for signs that a child is finding it difficult to hear, or if your voice is too loud, and adjust your volume control accordingly.

- Remember that children will disengage if the adult appears bored, preoccupied or uninterested.

- Be present in the moment with the young person. Just sitting close by can really aid recovery.

- Give the young person a safe space, and the time to sit, think and calm down naturally, devoid of any interference.

- Accept the young person's emotional state as it is. This is a powerful response that signifies you are not going to shame, humiliate or shut them down.

- Listen with empathy to what is being said, without being judgemental.

- Think about your facial expressions, body language and proximity to the child.

- Keep in mind that different responses are required at different times.

- A good starting point is to connect to the child's right-brain emotions first, before trying to access the left-brain logic and bring a child into balance.

- Never reject or abandon a child.

- Physical movement may be really beneficial.

- Teaching relaxation methods, such as mindfulness and breathing exercises, may be helpful in enabling a young person to calm intrusive thoughts.

- Providing distraction activities that are absorbing and require concentration may be helpful; for example, colouring, juggling, LEGO® building.

Finally, in the words of Ole Kirk Christiansen, master carpenter and founder of the LEGO® Group:

'LEG GODT' – Play well.

Appendix

Child observation form

Child's name:	Child's age:	Today's date:
Observer:	Setting:	The activity:

Reason for observation:

Time:	What happened: *Conversation, behaviour, movement, etc.*

Session log

Child's name:		Today's date:	Session number:
Theme this week:		Theme next week:	
Check-in activity:		Check-in response:	
Game:		Build:	
Model built:		Discussions:	
Concerns:		Notes:	
Holding in mind:			

Child cognitive behavioural therapy form

Child's name:	Today's date:
Situation/event: *Where was I?* *Who was with me?* *What happened?* *Was there a trigger?*	

Emotional response: *Arousal level 1–10*	Check-in before	Check-in after
Feelings: How was I feeling? Any physical sensations?		
Thoughts: What was I thinking? Were there any images in my head?		
Behaviours: What did I do? How did I cope?		
Outcomes: What happened afterwards?		

LEGO® vocabulary

Axle		A rod used to connect wheels, and to allow rotation of pieces. Comes in a variety of lengths.
Bracket		May overlap the smooth side of a brick, allowing the possibility of sideways model building.
Brick		Bricks form the basis of most models. They come in a variety of shapes, sizes, colours and textures.
Bushing		A small round axle-fitting that prevents items from slipping out of position.
Dalek		1×1 brick with knobs on four sides, allowing elements to connect in four directions.
Gear		A circular piece with jagged 'teeth' on the outer edge, and holes in the middle.
Headlight		Officially called an 'Erling' after the brick's inventor, but originally used for headlights on LEGO® cars.
Hinge		Hinges allow models to open up and fold back again, and allow an exact angle to be staged.
Hole		Bricks with holes are necessary to join parts of models together, using pegs or axles.
Jumper		Jumpers are brilliant for creating half-stud offset to a model.
Peg		A small peg that is used to connect beams and Technic pieces, via the holes.
Plate		Plates have studs on the top, but are three times thinner than bricks.
Round brick		Like a brick, but round, not square!
Slope		Fundamental for slicing a square edge, used primarily for roof-building.
Stud		The round raised bumps on top of bricks and plates, usually branded with the LEGO® name.
Tile		A tile is thin like a plate, but flat on top, and smooth, with no studs.

Glossary

Active listening	Involves more than just the act of listening carefully. It includes making sure that a young person feels safe and comfortable to talk, and requires the practitioner to take a genuine interest in the child, to observe body language and other non-verbal cues, in order to try to understand them.
Amygdala	Part of the limbic system that contributes to the detection of a threat.
Anxiety disorder	A mental health disorder in which feelings of intense worry and trepidation are exhibited, without apparent reason or logic, resulting in physiological arousal.
Arousal	Refers to the physiological state of readiness or general state of energy and excitement of a person's nervous system.
Attachment	The connection between a child and their primary care-giver.
Attunement	The feeling of being in harmony with another.
Brain plasticity	Refers to the brain's ability to change throughout life, for both better and worse. Biology, environment and experience all play a significant role in human brain plasticity.
Cerebral hemispheres	The two parts of the cerebrum (the main part of the brain), connected by the corpus callosum.
Congruence	Being yourself, even within a professional role. Not pretending and being aware of your own feelings and attitudes.
Corpus callosum	The part of the brain that allows communication between the two hemispheres of the brain. It is responsible for transmitting neural messages between both the right and left hemispheres.
Countertransference	A practitioner's emotional reaction, or 'felt' response, to a young person, through identification with the emotions, experiences or characteristics of the child.
Dissociation	When a child becomes so overwhelmed by their emotions or a particular situation that they detach and shut down as a maladaptive coping strategy.

Emotional intelligence	The ability to notice, evaluate, understand and express emotions accurately and appropriately, and to regulate them.
Empathy	The ability to understand and share the feelings of another, by connecting with something within you, that helps you to imagine what it would be like to be in that person's situation.
Externalising behaviours	When a child acts out loudly and aggressively, refusing to comply.
Fight/flight/freeze response	The main human, primitive and powerful survival reactions to imminent threat.
Flow	A wonderfully mindful and powerful building state, in which a child is relaxed, connected and most likely to talk openly. The challenge is not too excessive, causing anxiety, but neither is it insufficient, leading to boredom.
Hippocampus	The part of the limbic system thought to be the centre of emotion and involved in the formation of new memories and learning.
Hyper arousal	An involuntary physiological state where the body reaches a state of heightened anxiety. It is characterised by being easily startled, an elevated heart rate, slightly raised body temperature, sleep difficulties, irritability, outbursts of anger, difficulty concentrating and hypervigilance.
Hypervigilance	The state of feeling constantly 'on guard', primed and ready to respond, if threatened.
Hypo arousal	An involuntary physiological state where the body slows, or forcefully shuts down. This is not a calm or peaceful state, and is characterised by underresponsiveness to stimuli and environment. It may be perceived as boredom or apathy.
Internalising behaviours	When a child becomes withdrawn, quiet, shy, fearful, avoidant.
Left-brain hemisphere	Responsible for controlling the right side of the body. The more rational, logical side of the brain.
Mirroring	The attempt to hear, understand and reflect a young person's experience, through genuine interest, synchronicity of movement and focus on the child, to build a connection.

MOC	LEGO® speak for 'my own creation'. Meaning a model made from a person's own imagination, with no instructions.
Neuron	A cell in the nervous system designed to receive, process and carry signals from one place to another, around the many parts of the nervous system.
Right-brain hemisphere	Responsible for controlling the left side of the body. The more imaginative, creative side of the brain.
Self-awareness	Having a clear, conscious knowledge of one's own character, feelings, thoughts, motivation and beliefs.
Self-regulation	The ability to manage powerful emotions and remain on-task.
SEND	Special educational needs and disabilities.
Shame	A profound sense of separation from yourself and others. The threat, or experience of rejection, abandonment, disconnection and of not belonging.
Stress	Primarily a physical response, brought about by a state of mental/emotional strain or tension.
Transference	When a young person 'transfers' their thoughts and feelings from someone in their early life onto the practitioner, or when the past is brought into the present via a trigger, which is often a disproportionate response to a historical event.
Trauma	Occurs when a child has an experience, or repeated experiences, that leave them feeling unsafe and overwhelmingly fearful.
Unconditional positive regard	Complete love and acceptance of an individual by another with no conditions attached.
Window of tolerance	The level of arousal at which a child functions most successfully; unique to every individual.

Bibliography

Bowlby, J. (1988) *A Secure Base.* Abingdon: Routledge.

Briers, S. (2009) *Brilliant Cognitive Behavioural Therapy.* London: Pearson.

Brown, B. (2013) *RSA Short Dr Brené Brown on Empathy.* Accessed on 12/12/2017 at https://www.thersa.org/discover/videos/rsa-shorts/2013/12/Brene-Brown-on-Empathy.

Elkind, D. (2007) *The Power of Play: Learning What Comes Naturally.* Boston, MA: Da Capo Press.

Gerhardt, S. (2015) *Why Love Matters: How Affection Shapes a Baby's Brain.* Abingdon: Routledge (first edition 2004).

Hebb, D.O. (1949) *The Organization of Behavior.* Hoboken, NJ: John Wiley & Sons, Inc.

Hughes, D.A. (2011) *Attachment – Focused Family Therapy.* New York: W.W. Norton & Company.

Maslow, A. (1943) 'A theory of human motivation.' *Psychological Review 50,* 370–396.

Parten, M.B. (1932) 'Social participation among preschool children.' *Journal of Abnormal and Social Psychology 27,* 3, 243–269.

Rogers, C. (1991) *Client-Centred Therapy.* London: Constable.

Rosenberg, M. (1989) *Society and the Adolescent Self-Image.* Revised edition. Middletown, CT: Wesleyan University Press.

Shanker, S. and Barker, T. (2017) *Self-Reg: How to Help Your Child (and You) Break the Stress Cycle and Successfully Engage with Life.* New York: Penguin.

Siegel, D. and Payne Bryson, T. (2012) *The Whole-Brain Child.* New York: Bantam Books.

Thomsen, A. and Green, K. (2016) *Mood Monsters.* Accessed on 12/12/2017 at www.build-happy.co.uk.

Thomsen, A. and Green, K. (2017) *5 Ways to Well-Being.* Accessed on 12/12/2017 at www.build-happy.co.uk.

van der Kolk, B. (2014) *The Body Keeps the Score.* London: Penguin.

Vygotsky, L.S. (1978) *Mind in Society: Development of Higher Psychological Processes.* Cambridge, MA: Harvard University Press.

Index